LEISURE ARTS PRESENTS

THE SPIRIT OF CHRISTMAS

CREATIVE HOLIDAY IDEAS BOOK THIRTEEN

Christmas is celebrated in a multitude of ways around the world, but the true meaning of the holiday remains the same no matter where we are. In remembrance of our Saviour's birth, we offer our warmest wishes to family and friends and share moments that become cherished memories. Magnify the joy of the season in your own home with inventive ideas from this enchanting volume. Inside you'll find pages filled with decorating ideas for every style, handmade gifts with unique wrappings, and recipes for scrumptious foods that will delight one and all. So open your home and your heart to others — and enjoy an unforgettable Yuletide!

LEISURE ARTS, INC.
Little Rock, Arkansas

THE SPIRIT OF CHRISTMAS®
BOOK THIRTEEN

EDITORIAL STAFF

Vice President and Editor-in-Chief: Anne Van Wagner Childs
Executive Director: Sandra Graham Case
Design Director: Patricia Wallenfang Sowers
Test Kitchen Director/Foods Editor: Celia Fahr Harkey, R.D.
Editorial Director: Susan Frantz Wiles
Publications Director: Kristine Anderson Mertes
Creative Art Director: Gloria Bearden

PRODUCTION
DESIGN
Designers: Polly Tullis Browning, Cherece Athy Cooper,
   Cyndi Hansen, Sandra Spotts Ritchie, Billie Steward,
   Anne Pulliam Stocks, and Linda Diehl Tiano
Executive Assistant: Debra Smith
Craft Assistants: Diana Sanders Cates, Dani Martin, and
   Melanie Vaughan

FOODS
Assistant Foods Editor: Jane Kenner Prather
Test Kitchen Home Economist: Rose Glass Klein
Test Kitchen Coordinator: Nora Faye Taylor
Test Kitchen Assistants: Brandy Black Alewine,
   Camille T. Alstadt, and Donna Huffner Spencer

TECHNICAL
Managing Editor: Barbara McClintock Vechik
Senior Technical Writer: Susan McManus Johnson
Technical Writers: Sherry Solida Ford,
   Jennifer Potts Hutchings, Laura Lee Powell,
   Theresa Hicks Young, and Marley N. Washum
Technical Associates: Jennifer L. Hobbs, Charlotte Loftin,
   Candice Treat Murphy, and Kimberly Smith
Copy Editor: Susan Frazier
Production Assistant: Sharon Gillam

EDITORIAL
Managing Editor: Linda L. Trimble
Senior Associate Editor: Stacey Robertson Marshall
Associate Editors: Darla Burdette Kelsay and
   Janice Teipen Wojcik
Copy Editor: Terri Leming Davidson

ART
Book/Magazine Graphics Art Director: Diane Thomas
Senior Graphics Illustrator: Michael A. Spigner
Graphics Illustrator: Linda Chambers
Color Technician: Mark Hawkins
Photography Stylists: Beth Carter, Karen Smart Hall,
   Aurora Huston, and Christina Myers
Publishing Systems Administrator: Cynthia M. Lumpkin
Publishing Systems Assistant: Myra Means

PROMOTIONS
Managing Editor: Alan Caudle
Associate Editor: Steven M. Cooper
Designer: Dale Rowett
Art Director: Linda Lovette Smart

*"...and it was always said of him, that he knew how
to keep Christmas well, if any man alive possessed the
knowledge. May that be truly said of us, and all of us!"*

— From *A Christmas Carol* by Charles Dickens

BUSINESS STAFF

Publisher: Rick Barton
Vice President and General Manager: Thomas L. Carlisle
Vice President, Finance: Tom Siebenmorgen
Vice President, Retail Marketing: Bob Humphrey
Vice President, National Accounts: Pam Stebbins
Retail Marketing Director: Margaret Sweetin

General Merchandise Manager: Cathy Laird
Vice President, Operations: Brian U. Davis
Distribution Director: Rob Thieme
Retail Customer Service Manager: Wanda Price
Print Production Manager: Fred F. Pruss

Library of Congress Catalog Card Number 98-65188
International Standard Book Number 1-57486-128-X

10 9 8 7 6 5 4 3 2 1

TABLE OF CONTENTS

THE SIGHTS OF CHRISTMAS

Page 6

TABLE OF CONTENTS
(Continued)

THE TASTES OF CHRISTMAS

Page 116

THE SHARING OF CHRISTMAS

Page 94

THE
SIGHTS OF
CHRISTMAS

*Year after year, we are captivated
by the glimmering sights of
Christmas. Sparkling lights and
billowy bows evoke memories of
holidays past and remind us of the
glory of the season. You can create
your own traditional Yuletide
treasures with inventive ideas from
our exciting ensembles. Whether you
choose the rustic look of primitive
angels or a charming theme with
teddy bear chefs, you'll marvel at our
wonderful variety of projects. This
superb medley includes creative home
decor, ornaments and garlands for
the tree, as well as gift bags, stockings,
wreaths, and much, much more.
Make your home a tribute to the
season with fanciful decorations
from our fabulous collections!*

Keep Christmas in your ♥

e is where you hang your heart
Home is where

7

MAKE AN ENTRANCE

Give new meaning to the phrase "make an entrance" with creative entryway decor that's wonderfully entrancing! Begin with items borrowed from nature, such as evergreens, garlands of greenery, frosty snowballs, or luscious fruits; then use your imagination to develop a one-of-a-kind look. To create a sense of symmetry, arrange inviting decorations on either side of the doorway, or accessorize with a coordinating wreath or evergreen sprays. Instructions for creating three distinctive themes, including the farm-fresh style shown here, begin on page 12.

Even if you live in the middle of town, you can create a **Cozy Country Entrance** *(page 12)*. The wreath and garland combine rosy apples, checked ribbon, and galvanized stars for a charming provincial look. Complete the scene with rustic wooden reindeer, a weathered wheelbarrow, and buckets filled with country treasures.

For a **Winter Wonderland Entry** *(page 12)*, post **Cheerful Snowmen** *(page 13)* at the gate. They're sure to give guests a jolly welcome! A pair of slender artificial trees are wired together to form an impressive arch that 's quick to decorate with **Cheery Snowballs** *(page 13)* and store-bought "candy canes," snowflakes, and icicles.

Festooned with gleaming ribbons, faux fruit, and sprigs of greenery, elegant spiral trees stand sentry in this Renaissance-style **Della Robbia Entry Collection** *(page 12)*. The luxurious flourishes are repeated in the evergreen sprays that grace the double doors in a matched set. Draped atop the doorway, a fruited garland completes the ensemble.

11

COZY COUNTRY ENTRANCE
(Shown on pages 8 - 9)

Welcome family and friends to your home with this cozy country Christmas entryway.

The jaunty wreath is certain to catch the eye of those who come to call during this happy season. Artificial apples and greenery picks are wired to a 24" dia. silk evergreen wreath. A 6"w galvanized star ornament hangs at its center. The wreath is adorned with a pretty bow fashioned from $1^1/_2$"w red-and-white checked wired ribbon, and is hung from a length of the same ribbon.

An artificial miniature apple garland is wired along the boughs of a silk evergreen garland and draped across the doorway. Large imitation apples, 6"w and 14"w galvanized silver stars, and lengths of ribbon also decorate the swag. A cheery bow is nestled in its center.

Star-spangled woodland critters stand ready to welcome your guests. Ribbon "bow ties," greenery, and star ornaments adorn the necks of two rustic wooden "reindeer."

To complete the down-home setting, store-bought trees and artificial apples fill galvanized buckets, while an old-fashioned wheelbarrow totes a treasured quilt and lush poinsettias.

DELLA ROBBIA ENTRY COLLECTION
(Shown on page 11)

When guests come to your door during this glorious holiday season, greet them with an entryway inspired by Renaissance sculptors. The garland, door swags, and spiraled trees, heavy-laden with fruits and berries and draped in sparkling ribbons, create an aura of elegance.

To create each of our splendid tree sentries, we began by wiring faux fruit, including apples, pears, peaches, and grapes, along the boughs of a purchased eight-foot-tall spiral tree. For added color, sprigs of cedar, mistletoe, and berries, cut in 6" to 9" lengths, are interspersed throughout the limbs and secured with glue. Streamers are fashioned from $2^1/_2$"w gold and sheer plaid wired ribbons. For each streamer, we cut a 1 yard length of each ribbon and wired the ends to a floral pick. The streamers are then secured to the tree with the floral pick and arranged in splendid style. The tree is then topped with bows fashioned from both gold and plaid ribbons. As a symbol of hospitality, a large pineapple adds the crowning touch to our Della Robbia trees.

For each of our festive door sprays, we cut three 24" lengths from a silk evergreen garland. The cut lengths are wired together 9" from one end. Luscious artificial fruits, gilded mistletoe, and brilliant berries are wired along each branch. A cheerful bow adds the finishing touch.

Finally, to complete our grand ensemble, golden mistletoe is sprinkled throughout a second garland and accented with fanciful bows with delicate streamers. This handsome swag is gracefully draped over the exquisite doorway.

WINTER WONDERLAND ENTRY
(Shown on page 10)

Even if the snow isn't falling where you live, you can transform your front door into a winter wonderland with our playful snowmen and snowball-decorated arch. Covered with everything that makes Christmas merry, from sweet candy canes to crimson icicles and dazzling snowflakes, this darling arrangement, along with our frolicsome snowmen, is sure to delight young and old alike.

The tops of two nine-foot-tall artificial slim noble fir trees are wired together to form the inviting arch. Purchased glitter-covered snowflakes, red acrylic icicles, and artificial cherry picks are wired among the boughs. Red-and-white checked ribbon accents the wintry branches.

The Cheery Snowballs add a frosty accent to this playful arched gateway, and they won't melt even in the mildest of climes!

The doorway is flanked with a pair of ribbon-tied "candy canes." For each pair, two 25" artificial candy canes are crossed and wired together, then accented with a bright red bow.

The whimsical arch is positioned around the door and two 4' x 8' pieces of whitewashed fencing extend from each side. Two Cheerful Snowmen are standing by, ready to invite your loved ones across your threshold to enjoy your happy holiday hospitality.

CHEERFUL SNOWMEN (Shown on page 10)

For each snowman, you will need 6 yds. of ¹/₂" thick sheet foam, 15" x 42" piece of lightweight cardboard, 12"h flowerpot, stapler, fiberfill, mittens, low-temperature glue gun, hat, black craft foam, tracing paper, scarf, and one Cheery Snowball or 25" artificial candy cane.

1. Cut one 24" x 33" piece, two 16¹/₂" x 24" pieces, and three 24" x 50" pieces from sheet foam.
2. For body, overlapping short ends, wrap cardboard around flowerpot; staple to secure. With one long edge even with bottom of cardboard, wrap one 24" x 50" foam piece around flowerpot; staple at back to secure. Cut a wavy edge along one long edge of each remaining 24" x 50" foam piece. Layer and wrap around first foam piece; staple at back to secure. Staple front and back, then side edges of body together at top for neck.

3. For each arm, roll one 16¹/₂" x 24" piece of foam from long end to long end; staple to secure. Lightly stuff each mitten with fiberfill. Pull a mitten over one end of each arm; glue to secure.
4. For head, matching long edges, fold remaining piece of foam in half. With fold at top, match short edges to form a tube; staple to secure. Place hat over folded edge of head.
5. Trace eye, nose, mouth, and button patterns onto tracing paper. Using patterns, cut shapes from craft foam. Glue shapes to snowman.
6. Staple arms to neck. Staple head to neck and arms. Knot scarf around neck. Glue snowball or candy cane to one mitten.

CHEERY SNOWBALLS
(Shown on page 10)

For each snowball, you will need a drawing compass, ¹/₂" thick sheet foam, 2" dia. or 3" dia. plastic foam ball, and a white chenille stem.

1. For small snowball, use compass to draw a 9" dia. circle on sheet foam; cut out. Gather sheet foam around 2" dia. foam ball. Use stem to secure gathers.
2. For large snowball, follow Step 1 using 3" dia. foam ball and cutting a 12" dia. circle from sheet foam.

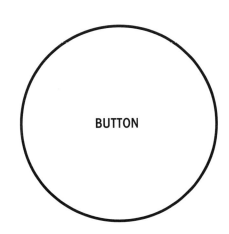

NOSE

BUTTON

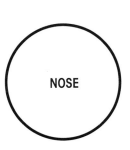

EYE

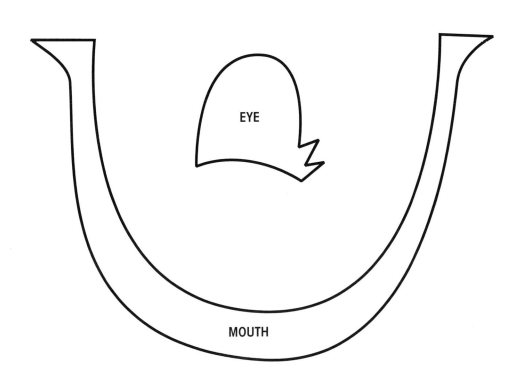

MOUTH

COOKING UP CHRISTMAS FUN

A spoonful of fun and a pinch of good cheer — our busy bears have the recipe for a jolly holiday right here! Create a wonderland of sweet sensations, including a candy-covered "gingerbread" house, a cheery hand-painted cookie plate, merry gift bags, and a festive tree covered with "beary" delightful decorations. With this array of tasty-looking treats, you'll have everything you need to "cook up" lots of Yuletide spirit on the evergreen and throughout your home. Easy-to-follow instructions for the charming projects shown here and on the following pages begin on page 18.

This **Bear Chef** *(page 19)* is hard at work decorating our sweet **Gingerbread House** *(page 21)*. The building is really a detergent box accented with cookies, candies, spray snow, and dimensional paint.

15

From the whimsical **Frosting Bowl Tree Topper** *(page 20)* shown on page 15 to the tree skirt shown opposite, our **Cooking Up Christmas Fun Tree** *(page 18)* has a whole lot of "baking" going on! **Bear Chefs** *(page 19)*, **House Cookie Ornaments** *(page 20)*, and **Coaster "Cookies"** *(page 21)* are accented by purchased wooden candy garland, small apple ornaments, and polka-dot baubles. **Frosting Bowls** *(page 18)* and **Spoon Ornaments** *(page 19)* look yummy dripping with dollops of "icing," and **Oven Mitt Ornaments** *(page 18)* and **Recipe Cards** *(page 18)* are the right ingredients for the baking theme.

Create a tasteful presentation with a **Painted Cookie Plate** *(page 21)*. It's a cinch to embellish a plain glazed plate using glass paint.

Busy little bear chefs are cooking up their own fun amid presents packaged in **Christmas Fun Gift Bags** (page 20) trimmed with cookie ornaments, wooden spoons, and miniature oven mitts. The **Christmas Fun Tree Skirt** (page 18) adds holiday flair with its peppy polka-dot fabric and rickrack trim.

COOKING UP CHRISTMAS FUN TREE
(Shown on page 15)

Teddy bear pastry chefs are here to help with your holiday baking! This fanciful tree is sweetened with wooden candy garland and sprinkled with small apple ornaments. Adding an extra dash of cheer to red glass ornaments, white dimensional paint is dotted over their shiny surfaces. Arranged below the bear-laden boughs is a colorful Christmas Fun Tree Skirt.

Paint, candy, and glitter transform purchased cork coasters and ordinary cardboard into delicious-looking Coaster "Cookies" (page 21) and House Cookie Ornaments (page 20). Oven Mitt Ornaments are a perfect fit for the baking theme.

Busy little Bear Chefs rise to the occasion with aprons, hats, and spoons. With cheerful Recipe Cards to guide them, these teddies really get into their work! They hop into the Frosting Bowls to get every last dollop of frosting. Super-simple Spoon Ornaments, with their acrylic frosting and bright bows, are sure to entice you into the cooking mood, too!

RECIPE CARDS
(Shown on page 16)

For each card, you will need tracing paper, 3" x 5" unruled index card, transfer paper, green wide-tip marker, and red and black permanent fine-point markers.

1. Trace recipe card pattern onto tracing paper. Use transfer paper to lightly transfer recipe and border to card.
2. Use green marker to draw patches along edges of card. Use red marker to draw "stitches" on patches and draw over border. Use black marker to draw over recipe.

CHRISTMAS FUN TREE SKIRT (Shown on page 17)

You will need two 46" squares of white fabric, string, thumbtack, green-and-white striped fabric for binding, green-and-white polka-dot fabric for border, and 8 yds. of red jumbo rickrack.

Note: Use a 1/2" seam allowance for all sewing.

1. For skirt front and lining, layer white fabric pieces with edges even. Using a 2" measurement for inside cutting line and a 20" measurement for outside cutting line, follow Steps 2 and 3 of **Cutting a Fabric Circle**, page 156, to cut skirt front and lining from white fabric; unfold.
2. For opening, cut from center to outer edge through both layers.
3. Stitching along all edges, baste skirt front and back together.
4. For border, make 4 yds. of 6"w bias strip from polka-dot fabric, piecing as necessary. Matching wrong sides and long edges, press border in half. Matching raw edges, pin border along outer edge of skirt. Easing to fit, sew border to skirt along folded edge of border, then along raw edges. Trim border ends even with opening edges.

OVEN MITT

FROSTING BOWLS
(Shown on page 16)

You will need white dimensional paint, shrinking plastic, a set of plastic mixing bowls, nail, and 8" lengths of craft wire.

1. Spread paint in a puddle over a sheet of shrinking plastic. Allow to dry. Peel paint off plastic. Use a small amount of paint to adhere half of dried paint inside bowl, allowing remaining half to hang over edge of bowl.
2. Repeat for each remaining bowl. Use nail to punch two holes 2" apart in sides of each bowl. Thread wire ends through holes and wire bowls to tree.

5. For binding, make 6 yds. of 2 1/2"w bias strip from striped fabric, piecing as necessary. Press one long edge of binding 1/2" to wrong side. Cut one 4 yd. length, one 13 1/2" length, and two 22" lengths from binding. Matching right sides and unpressed edge, sew binding along outer edge of skirt front. Fold binding over to skirt back. Sew pressed edge of binding to skirt; trim binding ends even with opening edges.
6. Sew rickrack to skirt front along edges of border and binding.
7. For skirt opening, press one short end of each 22" length of binding under 1/2". Aligning pressed ends with outer edge of skirt and matching right sides and long raw edges, sew bindings to opening edges. Fold bindings over to lining. Sew pressed edges of bindings to skirt. Trim bindings even with inner edges of skirt.
8. Press short ends of 13 1/2" length of binding under 1/2". Aligning pressed ends with opening edges of skirt, match right sides and long raw edges to sew binding to inner edge of skirt. Fold binding over to lining. Sew long pressed edge of binding to skirt.

OVEN MITT ORNAMENTS
(Shown on page 16)

For each ornament, you will need tracing paper, 6" x 10" piece each of fusible fleece and red-and-white striped fabric, fabric marking pen, and one 10" and one 5" length of 1/4"w double-fold bias binding.

1. Trace mitt pattern onto tracing paper; cut out.
2. Follow manufacturer's instructions to fuse fleece to wrong side of fabric.
3. Sew 10" length of binding to one long edge of fabric.
4. Matching right sides and bound edges, fold fabric in half. Use pattern and fabric marking pen to trace mitt onto fleece. Sew directly on drawn line to make mitt. Cut out mitt 1/4" from seamline. Clip curves and turn right side out.
5. For hanger, match short ends of remaining binding, forming a loop. Tack loop ends inside mitt.

Cooking up some
1 heap of holiday cheer
1 jumble of jolly bears
2 spoonfuls of sugar and spice
Mix "beary" well.
Christmas fun.

RECIPE CARD

BOY CHEF

You will need a 9"h jointed teddy bear, white fabric, tracing paper, brown and grey craft foam, hot glue gun, 12" of floral wire, red-and-white polka-dot fabric, craft glue, red baby rickrack, fabric marking pen, and a black permanent fine-point marker.

Note: Use a 1/4" seam allowance for all sewing unless otherwise indicated. Allow paint and glue to dry after each application.

1. From white fabric, cut a 3" x 7" piece for hatband and a 3" x 14" piece for hat crown. Matching wrong sides and long edges, press hatband in half. Beginning and ending 1/2" from short ends, baste 1/8" from each long edge of hat crown; pull threads to gather one long edge to 7" long.
2. Matching right sides, sew gathered edge of crown to raw edge of hatband. Matching right sides and raw edge, sew short ends together.
3. Pull threads to gather remaining edge of crown; tie thread ends. Sew along gathers to secure. Turn hat right side out.
4. Trace tiny oven mitt, chef's apron, spoon, pancake turner, and turner handle patterns onto tracing paper; cut out.
5. Leaving straight edges open and using polka-dot fabric and mitt pattern, follow **Sewing Shapes**, page 156, to sew mitt. Fold straight edge 1/4" to wrong side and press.
6. Using white fabric and chef's apron pattern, follow **Sewing Shapes** to sew apron. Turn right side out; press. Sew opening closed.

SPOON ORNAMENTS
(Shown on page 16)

For each ornament, you will need white dimensional paint, wooden spoon, 14" of 5/8"w red grosgrain ribbon, 6" of floral wire, and a hot glue gun.

1. For frosting, paint half of spoon bowl.
2. For hanger, glue one end of floral wire to back of handle.
3. Tie ribbon into a bow. Glue bow to front of spoon.

7. For pocket, cut two 2" x 3" pieces of white fabric. Matching right sides and raw edges and leaving an opening for turning, sew pocket pieces together. Turn right side out; press. Sew opening closed.
8. Use marker to write "Seasoned Greetings" on pocket. Position pocket on apron front. Stitch in place along side and bottom edges of pocket.
9. Glue one length of rickrack along top edge of apron and one length along bottom curve of apron; trim glued rickrack ends even with apron edges. Cut two 22" lengths of rickrack. Leaving ends free for ties, glue center of one length along each underarm edge, covering glued rickrack ends. Tie apron on bear.
10. Using patterns, cut spoon, pancake turner, and turner handle from craft foam. Use marker to draw circle for bowl of spoon and dots for brads on turner handle. Glue turner handle to pancake turner. Place spoon and pancake turner in apron pocket.
11. Glue hat to bear. Place mitt on bear's paw.
12. If hanger is desired, wrap wire around waist; twist to secure. Twist ends together to form a loop.

GIRL CHEF
You will need a 9"h jointed teddy bear, white fabric for hat, tracing paper, brown craft foam, hot glue gun, 12" of floral wire, red- or green-and-white striped fabric, red- or green-and-white polka-dot fabric, craft glue, 3/8"w red or green grosgrain ribbon, 1 5/8"h wooden gingerbread man, and white dimensional paint.

Note: Use a 1/4" seam allowance for all sewing unless otherwise indicated. Allow paint and glue to dry after each application.

1. Follow Steps 1 - 3 of Boy Chef to make hat.
2. Trace spoon pattern onto tracing paper; cut out. Using pattern, cut one spoon from brown craft foam. Use dimensional paint to add "frosting" to spoon and wooden gingerbread man.
3. For apron bib, cut a 1 1/2" x 3 1/2" piece of striped fabric. For apron skirt, cut a 5 1/2" x 8 1/2" piece of polka-dot fabric.
4. Press long edges of apron bib 1/4" to wrong side. Matching wrong sides and short edges, fold and press bib in half.
5. Press short edges of apron skirt 1/4" to wrong side. Matching wrong sides and long edges, fold and press skirt in half. Baste long raw edges. Pull threads, drawing up gathers to measure 4 1/2". Centering bib on skirt, sew bib to skirt. Press seam allowance toward skirt.
6. Leaving ends free for ribbon ties, use craft glue to glue center of a 22" length of ribbon over seam allowance. Cut two 16" lengths of ribbon. Glue one end of each ribbon to back corner of bib.
7. For hair bow, cut a 3/4" x 14" strip of fabric. Tie strip into a bow around one ear. Glue hat to opposite ear. Glue gingerbread man and spoon to bear. Tie apron on bear.
8. If hanger is desired, wrap wire around waist; twist to secure. Twist ends together to form a loop.

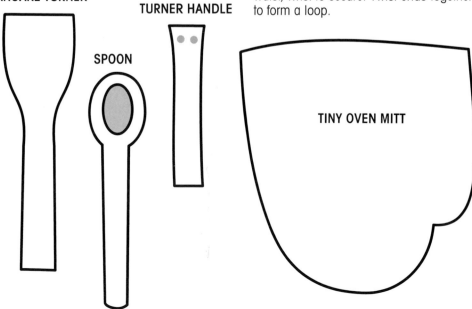

CHEF'S APRON

PANCAKE TURNER

SPOON

TURNER HANDLE

TINY OVEN MITT

HOUSE COOKIE ORNAMENTS
(Shown on page 16)

For each ornament, you will need tracing paper, corrugated cardboard, white acrylic paint, hot glue gun, items to decorate house (we used candy canes, peppermints, spice drops, round and square sour candies, shaped Christmas candy, bell-shaped candy, and candy-coated chocolate pieces), white dimensional paint, 2"h gingerbread man cookie, spray snow, and 8" of $5/8$"w red grosgrain ribbon.

1. Trace house pattern onto tracing paper; cut out. Use pattern to cut house from cardboard. Paint eaves, doors, windows, and snowdrifts with acrylic paint.
2. Arrange and glue candies to house. Use dimensional paint to outline eaves, door, candies, and details on gingerbread man cookie. Glue cookie to ornament. Spray ornament with snow.
3. For hanger, fold ribbon in half forming a loop. Glue ribbon ends to back of ornament.

CHRISTMAS FUN GIFT BAGS (Shown on page 17)

GINGERBREAD COOKIE GIFT BAG
You will need a 6"w x 11"h brown paper lunch bag, 12" square of red- or green-and-white polka-dot fabric, hot glue gun, House Cookie Ornament without hanger, hole punch, and $3/8$"w red or green grosgrain ribbon.

1. Glue ornament to front of paper bag. Roll top edges of bag $1 1/2$" to outside. Place gift in bag. Place fabric in bag to cover gift.
2. Holding bag closed, punch a hole through each top corner. Cut two 12" lengths of ribbon. Thread one ribbon length through holes in each side of bag; tie ribbon ends into bows.

SPOON GIFT BAG
You will need a 6"w x 11"h brown paper lunch bag, 12" square of red or green polka-dot fabric, hot glue gun, red- or green-and-white striped fabric, paper-backed fusible web, one Spoon Ornament without hanger (page 19), jumbo white rickrack, and two $3/4$" red or white buttons.

1. Fuse web to wrong side of each fabric. Matching bottom and side edges of bag, fuse a 6" x 9" piece of polka-dot fabric to front of bag. Matching top and side edges of bag, fuse a 3" x 6" piece of striped fabric to top back of bag.
2. Beginning $3 1/2$" below front top edge of bag, glue a 20" length of rickrack along side and bottom edges of bag front. Place gift in bag. Fold top of bag $2 1/2$" to front; glue to secure.
3. Overlapping ends, glue a 20" length of rickrack along edges of striped fabric. Glue one button to each corner of flap. Glue ornament to bag front.

"SEASONED GREETINGS" GIFT BAG
You will need a corrugated paper bag (we used an $8 1/2$"w x $10 1/4$"h bag), $3 5/8$" x $5 5/8$" piece of white card stock, red permanent medium-point marker, two $3 5/8$" and two $5 5/8$" lengths of green jumbo rickrack, hot glue gun, four $3/4$" dia. red buttons, Oven Mitt Ornament (page 18), three wrapped hard spearmint candies, tissue paper, and two safety pins.

1. For tag, use marker to write "Seasoned Greetings" on card stock. Glue rickrack along edges of tag. Glue buttons to corners. Stuff mitt with tissue paper. Place candies inside mitt.
2. Glue tag to front of bag. Use safety pins to pin ornament to bag.

FROSTING BOWL TREE TOPPER
(Shown on page 15)

You will need white dimensional paint, shrinking plastic, a plastic mixing bowl (we used a 9" dia. bowl), craft knife, cutting mat, nail, two 8" lengths of craft wire, two Bear Chefs (page 19), long wooden spoon, and a hot glue gun.

1. Follow Step 1 of Frosting Bowls (page 18) to make one bowl. On the same side as dried paint, use a craft knife to cut a hole in bottom of bowl to fit top of tree.
2. Place bears inside bowl; mark placement for each bear on bowl. Remove bears. Use nail to poke two holes 2" apart at each mark. Thread wire through holes and wire bears inside bowl. Place spoon in bowl; glue to secure.
3. Place bowl on tree.

HOUSE

COASTERS

COASTER "COOKIES"
(Shown on page 16)

For four ornaments, you will need tracing paper; yellow, red, green, and brown card stock; craft glue; a set of four 4" dia. purchased cork coasters with raised rims; white dimensional paint; spray-on glitter; craft stick; eight 20" lengths of 1/8"w green-and-white polka-dot satin ribbon; and a hot glue gun.

1. Trace coaster patterns onto tracing paper; cut out. Using patterns, cut shapes from card stock. Use craft glue to glue one shape to center of each coaster.
2. Use dimensional paint to outline shapes and add details to coaster. Apply glitter to coasters.
3. Use craft stick to apply dimensional paint to rims of coasters.
4. For each hanger, place two ribbon lengths together; knot ends together. Fold doubled ribbon in half. Use hot glue to glue fold at top back of ornament. Tie ends together 3" from ornament.

PAINTED COOKIE PLATE
(Shown on page 17)

You will need tracing paper; graphite paper; 10" dia. glazed white plate with 1 5/8"w rim; white, pink, red, green, brown, and black permanent enamel glass paint; paint conditioner; paint sealer; and paintbrushes.

Note: Allow paint to dry after each application unless otherwise indicated.

1. Follow manufacturer's instructions to apply conditioner to plate. Trace plate border pattern four times onto tracing paper; cut out. Arrange patterns to fit plate rim; tape together. Use graphite paper to transfer border to plate rim.
2. Paint ribbons green. Paint hearts brown and candy canes red. Paint lollipop stick white and lollipop candy pink. While pink paint is still wet, shade lollipop white.
3. Use graphite paper to transfer detail lines over dried paint. Paint centers of heart cookies white. Paint white stripes on candy canes. Paint red stripes on lollipop stick. Use red paint to outline swirls on lollipop candy. Use black paint to outline ribbons and add knots above ribbon ends.
4. Follow manufacturer's instructions to apply sealer to plate.

GINGERBREAD HOUSE
(Shown on page 14)

You will need tracing paper, lightweight corrugated cardboard, transfer paper, 5 1/4" x 8 3/4" x 7" box (we used a 92 ounce detergent box), hot glue gun, white acrylic paint, paintbrush, items to decorate house (we used miniature vanilla wafers, sugar wafers, butter cookies, hard candies, candy canes, gumdrops, chewy candy shapes, candy-coated fruit chews, red licorice whips, and bell-shaped candy), white dimensional paint, and spray snow.

Note: Allow paint and spray snow to dry after each application.

1. Trace house front, door, and window patterns onto tracing paper; cut out. Using house front/back pattern, cut house front and house back from cardboard. Cut two 7" x 9" pieces of cardboard for house sides. Cut two 4" x 9" pieces of cardboard for roof. Cut one 8" x 10" piece of cardboard for base.
2. Use transfer paper to transfer door to front and two windows to each side.
3. Center and glue bottom of box to base. Glue front, back, and sides to box. Glue roof pieces to house sides; glue top edges together.
4. Use acrylic paint to paint roof and door. Glue cookies and candies to house as desired.
5. Use dimensional paint to outline windows, cookies, and candies, and to fill in areas between cookies and candies.
6. Apply snow to house.

DOOR

HOUSE FRONT/BACK

WINDOW

PLATE BORDER

21

A
VICTORIAN
COLLECTION

Re-create the romantic
ambience of days gone by
with ideas from our Victorian
collection. Peeking from among
the evergreen branches are
cherub-faced children and fancy
decorative cones filled with
delectable treats. Add a tender
touch with silver-spoon nosegays
and crocheted teacups brimming
with silky crimson roses. You'll
also discover elegant accents for
the home, such as a patchwork
stocking pieced with luxurious
fabrics and a swag of holiday
greenery embellished with
beaded stars. Instructions for
the projects shown here and
on the following pages
begin on page 28.

Our **Victorian Christmas Tree** *(page 28)* is an enchanting tribute to days of old. **Victorian Girl Ornaments** *(page 31)* and **Framed Postcards** *(page 30)* look divine dressed in scraps of velvet and frilly trims. Embellished with ribbon, beads, and faux flowers, **Rose Ornaments** *(page 29)* and **Cherub Ornaments** *(page 31)* complement **Tussie Mussies** *(page 30)* made with antique silver spoons as handles. **Gilded Cone Ornaments** *(page 30)*, **Teacup Nosegays** *(page 28)*, and **Beaded Stars** *(page 29)* are eye-catching alternatives to ordinary ornaments. Sprinkled among these timeless trims are purchased bead garlands, jeweled ornaments, gold ribbon, and metallic glass baubles.

Set a beautiful place at your holiday table with a fanciful **Tussie Mussie** *(page 30)* created by gathering a paper doily and a few ribbon roses around an old silver spoon.

Accent the mantel with an ornate **Crazy-Patch Stocking** *(page 28)* fashioned from pieces of vintage-look fabrics, delicate lace, and dainty ribbon. An evergreen garland dressed up with beaded stars gives extra pizzazz.

In the tradition of Christmases past, a ribbon-festooned **Kissing Ball** *(page 30)* will add a little romantic excitement to the season.

Create beautiful packages using shimmering paper and ribbons, and then top them off with **Victorian Girl Ornaments** *(page 31)* and **Cherub Ornaments** *(page 31)*.

Gilded Cone Ornaments *(page 30)* are as pretty as the treats they hold. Fill them with gourmet chocolates for elegant party favors.

A lovely covered **Scrapbook and Memory Pages** *(page 29)* provide a fun and decorative way to record treasured holiday memories.

VICTORIAN CHRISTMAS TREE
(Shown on page 23)

Imagine this wonderful tribute to early Christmas trees as the focal point of your holiday gatherings! Topped with an exquisite gold bow, this very Victorian tree radiates the warmth and elegance of a time gone by. The 7-foot blue spruce is skirted with red velvet, wrapped with glittering beaded garland, and draped with gold ribbon.

You'll hear lots of "oohs" and "aahs" as your guests discover the silver spoon Tussie Mussies (page 30) with their sweet ribbon roses and the candy-filled Gilded Cone Ornaments (page 30) topped with beaded hangers.

Cozy Teacup Nosegays are purchased crocheted cups holding dried rosebuds afloat in gold ribbon. You can make dozens of these beauties in a snap! Glass ball ornaments and purchased pearl icicles also complement the handmade creations.

Clever Victorian Girl Ornaments (page 31) are adorably trimmed in velvet, bows, and artificial fur. Cherub Ornaments (page 31) and Rose Ornaments feature sweet faces peeking out from leaves and blossoms.

Precious little ones also appear on Framed Postcards (page 30). To make them, color photocopies of antique cards are embellished with felt, velvet, and holly. Placed in golden frames and hanging from colorful bows, they're ready to bring the pleasures of Christmases past to your holidays.

TEACUP NOSEGAYS
(Shown on page 24)

For each teacup, you will need eight 2¹/₂" lengths of floral wire, eight dried rose buds, hot glue gun, 1¹/₂" square of floral foam, purchased crocheted teacup (we used a teacup with a 3¹/₂" dia. rim), 12" of 2¹/₂"w gold mesh wired ribbon, and eight 1¹/₂"w velvet leaves.

1. Insert one piece of floral wire into base of each rosebud; glue in place. Glue floral foam in bottom of cup.
2. Glue both ends and center of ribbon to floral foam.
3. Insert leaves into foam along rim of cup. Bend leaves down over rim. Insert one rose through ribbon into center of foam. Insert remaining roses into foam between ribbon and leaves.

CRAZY-PATCH STOCKING (Shown on page 25)

You will need tracing paper, 12" x 18" piece of red velvet, three 12" x 18" pieces of unbleached muslin, assorted velvet and print fabric scraps for stocking front, decorative trims (we used braid, lace, pre-strung beads, seed and bugle beads, lace motif, crocheted doily, brass charms, jeweled button, embroidery floss, and silk ribbon), seam ripper, 2 yds. of ¹/₄" dia. gold cord with lip, pressing cloth, and ³/₈" dia. gold cord.

1. Aligning arrows and dotted lines, trace stocking top and stocking bottom patterns, page 92, onto tracing paper. Draw a second line ¹/₄" outside first line. Cut out pattern along outer line. Using pattern, cut one stocking back from red velvet and three stocking shapes from muslin for lining pieces and stocking front foundation.
2. Cut a five-sided piece from one of the assorted fabric scraps; place right side up on center of stocking front foundation (**Fig. 1**).

Fig. 1

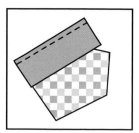

3. Matching right sides and one straight edge of five-sided piece, place a second piece on the first. Stitch through all layers ¹/₄" from matched edges (**Fig. 2**). Flip second piece to right side and press (**Fig. 3**).

Fig. 2

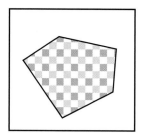

Fig. 3

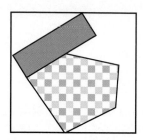

4. Referring to **Figs. 4** and **5**, continue to add pieces, stitch, flip, and press until pieces extend at least ¹/₄" past all edges of foundation.

Fig. 4

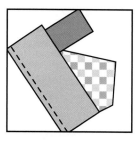

Fig. 5

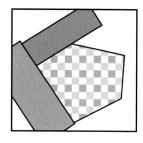

5. Carefully trim pieced front even with outer edges of foundation.
6. Using embroidery floss or silk ribbon, follow **Embroidery Stitches**, page 158, and **Ribbon Embroidery**, page 159, to add embroidery to seamlines and individual pieces. Machine or hand stitch trims along remaining seamlines. To finish ends of lace, braid, or pre-strung beads, use seam ripper to remove a few stitches from adjacent seamline; insert raw end of trim into opening. Blindstitch opening closed.
7. Match lip of ¹/₄" dia. cord to raw edges on right side of stocking front; baste in place along sides and bottom. Trim cord ends even with top edge. Matching right sides and leaving top edges open, use zipper foot to sew front and back of stocking together as close to cord as possible. Clip curves and turn stocking right side out.

CRAZY-PATCH STOCKING
(continued)

8. Matching edges and overlapping cord ends at heel side, sew lip of cord around top of right side of stocking. Use pressing cloth to press seam allowance to inside of stocking.

9. For lining, leaving top edges open, sew muslin for lining pieces together; do not turn. Use pressing cloth to press top edge of lining 1/4" to wrong side. Insert lining in stocking. Hand sew pressed edge of lining to seam allowance of stocking.

10. For hanger, fold 12" of 3/8" dia. cord in half. Knot cord 2" from fold. Fray cord ends; sew knot to stocking.

ROSE ORNAMENTS
(Shown on page 24)

For each ornament, you will need spray adhesive, color photocopy of desired face (page 33), poster board, 2 3/4"w sheer gold ribbon, hot glue gun, red silk rose with rosebud and leaves, and 10" of floral wire.

1. Apply spray adhesive to wrong side of photocopy; smooth onto poster board. Cut out.

2. Tie gold ribbon into a bow with two 5" loops and two 2 1/2" streamers. Arrange and glue rosebud, leaves, and rose to bow. Glue face to center of rose.

3. For hanger, bend wire in half; glue ends to back of ornament.

BEADED STARS
(Shown on page 24)

For each star, you will need 15" of floral wire and 25 each of 8mm gold and silver beads.

Thread beads onto wire. Twist ends together to secure; trim ends. Bend wire to form star shape.

SCRAPBOOK AND MEMORY PAGES (Shown on page 27)

SCRAPBOOK
You will need a scrapbook with post-and-screw binding, batting, hot glue gun, tracing paper, velvet, unbleached muslin, scraps of assorted velvets and print fabrics for scrapbook front, decorative trims (we used pre-strung beads, lace, braids, brass charms, embroidery floss, old jewelry pieces, seed and bugle beads, a lace medallion, a crocheted doily, and silk ribbon), seam ripper, craft knife, cutting mat, 2 yds. of 1/4" dia. gold cord with lip, and poster board.

Note: Allow glue to dry after each application.

1. Remove front cover and back cover from scrapbook. Draw around each cover on batting. Cut out batting along drawn lines.

2. Glue one batting piece each to outside of front and back covers. Draw around front cover on tracing paper. Cut out pattern 4" outside drawn lines. Using pattern, cut three pieces of velvet for back and inside covers and one piece of muslin for front cover foundation.

3. For front cover, follow Steps 2 - 6 of Crazy-Patch Stocking to piece and embellish front cover foundation.

4. Center front cover of scrapbook batting side down over wrong side of front cover foundation. Fold corners of pieced foundation diagonally over corners of cover; glue in place. Fold edges of pieced foundation over edges of cover; glue in place. Use craft knife to carefully cut an "X" in fabric for each post binding. Repeat for back cover using a piece of velvet.

5. Trimming to fit, glue lip of cord to wrong side of front cover along top, opening side, and bottom edges; trim cord end.

6. For each inside cover, measure width between opening side edge and crease at spine; measure height. Cut a piece from poster board the determined measurements. Center poster board on wrong side of one velvet piece for inside covers. Fold corners of velvet diagonally over corners of poster board; glue in place. Fold edges of velvet over edges of poster board; glue in place. Glue covered poster board to inside covers of scrapbook. Reassemble scrapbook.

MEMORY PAGES
You will need 14-carat gold paint, silk sponge, decorative tissue paper, spray adhesive, parchment velum, acid-free pages to fit scrapbook, dark green acid-free paper, glue stick, decorative-edge craft scissors, decorative photograph corners, 6" of 5/8"w gold ribbon, craft glue, tracing paper, transfer paper, and gold paint pen.

Note: Allow paint and glue to dry after each application.

1. Use gold paint and follow Sponge Painting, page 157, to paint edges of stacked pages. Sponge paint a 1/2"w strip along opening edge of each page.

2. Cut a sheet of tissue paper 1" smaller than page. Apply spray adhesive to wrong side of tissue paper; smooth onto page.

3. For photograph border, cut parchment or dark green paper 1" to 1 1/2" wider than photograph. Use glue stick to glue border to page. If double border is desired, use craft scissors to cut coordinating paper 1" smaller than outer border. Use glue stick to glue inner border to outer border.

4. Use glue stick to glue photographs to borders; glue photograph corners to borders and photographs. Tie a knot in center of ribbon. Use craft glue to glue knot of ribbon to border.

5. If desired, trace edging patterns, this page, onto tracing paper. Use transfer paper to transfer designs to borders. Use gold pen to draw over designs.

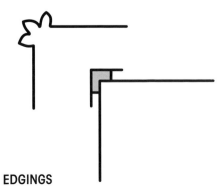

EDGINGS

GILDED CONE ORNAMENTS
(Shown on page 26)

For four paper cones, you will need one 16" square each of paper-backed fusible web and cream-and-gold print fabric, string, pencil, thumbtack, poster board, hot glue gun, 1/8" dia. hole punch, 10" of floral wire, assorted silver and pearl beads, four silver bump chenille stems, four gold cherub charms, 1/8"w burgundy satin ribbon, four 2 1/2"w x 7"h cellophane bags, desired candies, and 1/4"w gold ribbon.

1. Fuse web to wrong side of fabric. Fold fabric in half from top to bottom and again from left to right. Tie one end of string to pencil. Insert thumbtack through string 14" from pencil. Insert thumbtack in fabric; keeping string taut, mark cutting line (**Fig. 1**). Cut out circle along drawn line. Cut along each fold to cut circle into quarters.

Fig. 1

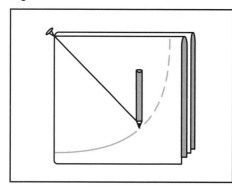

2. Fuse each quarter-circle to poster board. Cut out quarter-circles along edges of fabric.
3. For each ornament, shape one quarter-circle into a cone; glue overlapped edges together at back.
4. For handle, punch a hole in each side of cone 1/2" below top edge. Thread end of floral wire through one hole; bend wire to secure. Thread beads onto wire to cover 8" of wire. Thread remaining end of wire through remaining hole; bend wire to secure.
5. Trimming to fit, glue one chenille stem around cone 1/2" from top.
6. Glue charm to front of cone. Tie two 20" lengths of burgundy ribbon together into a bow around each side of handle.
7. Place cellophane bag in cone. Fill bag with candy. Tie gold ribbon into a bow around top of bag.

TUSSIE MUSSIES
(Shown on page 25)

For each tussie mussie, you will need one 10" and one 18" length of 1 1/2"w burgundy and purple variegated wired ribbon, 24" of 1 3/4"w dark rose wired ribbon, thread to match wired ribbons, 6" dia. ecru paper doily, hot glue gun, silver spoon, artificial greenery sprigs, artificial leaf, gold berry stem, wired pearl sprig, 24" of 1 1/2"w burgundy ribbon with gold foil edges, 16" of 1/8" dia. silver twist cord, floral wire, and wire cutters.

1. Using wired ribbons, follow **Making Ribbon Roses**, page 157, to make three roses.
2. Cut doily from outer edge to center. Overlapping cut edges 5", shape doily into a cone; glue to secure. Trim 1/2" from point of cone.
3. Insert handle of spoon into cone. Glue bowl of spoon to doily. Arrange roses, greenery, berry stem, and pearl sprig in doily; glue to secure.
4. Use gold-edged ribbon and follow **Making a Bow**, page 156, to make a bow with four 4" loops and two 3" streamers. Tie cord into a bow; knot cord ends. Glue cord bow to ribbon bow. Glue ribbon bow to spoon handle at small end of cone. For hanger, bend an 8" length of wire in half; glue bend of wire to back of handle.

FRAMED POSTCARDS (Shown on pages 23 and 24)

For each framed piece, you will need a color photocopy of desired postcard (page 33), spray adhesive, mat board to fit in frame, tracing paper, ecru felt, 2"w red velvet ribbon, items to decorate postcard (we used artificial greenery and berries, red embroidery floss, 7/8"w cream sheer ribbon, thread, and gold seed beads), thick craft glue, silver glitter dimensional paint, 5" x 7" gold frame, one yd. of 1 1/2"w striped wired ribbon, 10" of floral wire, and a hot glue gun.

Note: Use craft glue for all gluing unless otherwise indicated. Allow glue and paint to dry after each application.

KISSING BALL
(Shown on page 26)

You will need spray adhesive, 4" dia. plastic foam ball, sheet moss, wire cutters, 28 silk rosebud stems, artificial boxwood garland, ten 7" lengths and one 22" length of 5/8"w gold mesh wired ribbon, floral pins, three 22" lengths of 7/8"w burgundy wired ribbon with gold edges, 5" gold tassel, gold acrylic paint, and a paintbrush.

1. Apply spray adhesive to foam ball. Cover ball with sheet moss. Using wire cutters, trim stems of rosebuds to 1 1/2". Spacing evenly around ball, insert stems in ball.
2. Cut stems from garland. Filling spaces between rosebuds, insert stems into ball.
3. Form a 2" dia. loop in one end of each 7" length of ribbon. Spacing evenly around ball, use floral pins to pin loops to ball.
4. Pulling wire on one side of ribbon, gather two burgundy ribbons and 22" gold ribbon into circles; twist wires to secure. Use floral pin to pin one burgundy circle and tassel to bottom of ball. Layer and pin remaining circles to top of ball.
5. For hanger, fold remaining ribbon length in half. Insert floral pin 6" from fold and pin to top of ball.
6. Lightly brush edges of leaves and roses with gold paint; allow to dry.

1. Cut out photocopy along card edges. Apply spray adhesive to wrong side of photocopy; smooth onto mat board.
2. Trace areas of design to be covered with felt or ribbon onto tracing paper; cut out. Using patterns, cut out shapes. Arrange and glue shapes to photocopy.
3. Embellish photocopy as desired. Use dimensional paint to add details to photocopy.
4. Mount picture in frame. Tie wired ribbon into a bow with two 4" loops and two 12" streamers. Glue streamers of bow to back of frame.
5. For hanger, bend floral wire in half. Use hot glue to glue wire ends to back of frame.

CHERUB ORNAMENTS
(Shown on page 24)

For each ornament, you will need color photocopy of desired cherub face (pages 32 and 33), spray adhesive, poster board, 6" of 3"w sheer copper wired ribbon, hot glue gun, 14" of ⁵⁄₈"w green wired ribbon, gilded artificial leaves, artificial berry stem, 15mm star sequin, and 8" of floral wire.

1. Cut cherub from photocopy. Apply spray adhesive to wrong side of cherub. Smooth cherub onto poster board; cut out.
2. Matching wired edges, fold copper ribbon in half. Gathering to fit and gluing wired edges to back of cherub, glue copper ribbon along bottom edge of cherub. Tie green ribbon into a bow. Glue bow to front of cherub.
3. Arrange and glue leaves to back of cherub. Trimming to fit, glue berry stem to cherub for halo; glue sequin to halo.
4. For hanger, bend floral wire into a "U" shape; glue ends to back of ornament.

GIRL A

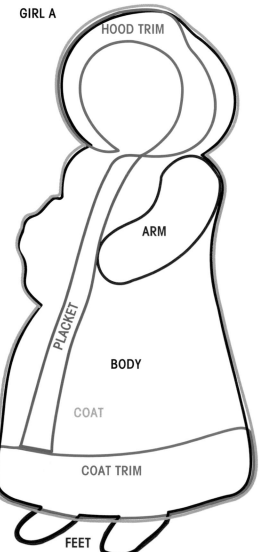

VICTORIAN GIRL ORNAMENTS (Shown on page 24)

GIRL A
You will need tracing paper, poster board, green crushed velvet, 3" of 1"w red velvet ribbon, ecru felt, ¹⁄₂" square of artificial fur for muff, color photocopy of Face A (page 32), spray adhesive, craft glue, 14" of ¹⁄₄"w gold trim, 6" of ⁵⁄₈"w burgundy ribbon, burgundy thread, and 3-ply gold cord.

1. Trace Girl A patterns separately onto tracing paper; cut out. Using patterns, cut body and arm from poster board; coat, arm, and hood from green velvet; feet from red velvet ribbon; and hood trim, placket, and coat trim from felt.
2. Cut face from photocopy. Apply spray adhesive to wrong side of face. Position and smooth face onto poster board body.
3. Use craft glue to glue velvet arm to poster board arm. Overlapping as necessary, arrange and glue remaining shapes to body. Glue gold trim along edges of coat trim and hood trim.
4. For bow, crisscrossing ends, make a 2" loop in center of burgundy ribbon; flatten loop. Pinch center of loop and tightly wrap thread around center of bow; knot thread ends at back. Glue bow to coat.
5. For hanger, twist two 6" lengths of gold cord together; fold in half. Glue cord ends to back of ornament.

GIRL B
You will need tracing paper, poster board, color photocopy of Face B and hand (page 32), craft glue, red thread, scrap of red velveteen for dress, 1³⁄₈"w red velvet ribbon, 2³⁄₄"w sheer gold wired ribbon, ¹⁄₂"w gold looped braid, 1¹⁄₂"w burgundy satin-edge sheer ribbon, artificial greenery sprig, decorative glass bead, 4mm red pearl beads, and 3-ply gold cord.

1. Trace Girl B patterns, page 32, separately onto tracing paper; cut out. Using patterns, cut body and arm from poster board, dress and arm from velveteen, and feet from red velvet ribbon.
2. Cut face and hand from photocopy. Apply spray adhesive to wrong side of face and hand; position and smooth face onto poster board body. Smooth hand onto poster board; cut out. Trimming to fit, glue braid to wrist.
3. Overlapping as necessary, arrange and glue shapes to body. Glue wrist to arm.
4. Trimming to fit, glue braid down front of dress. Glue arm to body.
5. Cut one 6" and one 10" length from gold wired ribbon. Gathering to fit, glue 10" length along bottom of dress and 6" length along edge of neck.
6. Glue red beads to braid on dress.
7. Tuck greenery under hand; glue in place.
8. For bow, crisscrossing ends, make a 2" loop in center of burgundy ribbon; flatten loop. Pinch center of loop and tightly wrap thread around center of bow; knot thread ends at back.
9. Glue bow to girl's hair. Glue one or two glass beads to bow.
10. For hanger, twist two 6" lengths of gold cord together; fold in half. Glue cord ends to back of ornament.

31

GIRL B

BODY

DRESS

ARM

FEET

FACE A

HAND

FACE B

The face and hand designs on this page are copyright free and may be photocopied for personal use.

CHERUB FACE

The designs on this page are copyright free and may be photocopied for personal use.

CHERUB FACE

ROSE ORNAMENT FACES

POSTCARDS

REDWORK REVIVAL

This charming collection of old-fashioned redwork embroidery reflects the current revival of a crisp, clean Scandinavian style of outlining simple designs in red. It's a wonderful way to spread seasonal cheer to the bedroom! If your room is too small for a full-size tree, don't worry — just stitch fewer ornaments and decorate a tabletop tree. You'll find everything you need to make your Yuletide merry, from personalized stockings, tree ornaments, and pillowcases to a table topper that wishes a Merry Christmas to all. We've even captured the charm of redwork in a lace-trimmed alphabet sampler. Instructions begin on page 38.

Sewn from red and white cotton ticking, our **Personalized Stockings** *(page 38)* feature embroidered cuffs fashioned from a linen tablecloth. *(Opposite)* Four festive designs are embroidered on muslin to create the stuffed **Pillow Ornaments** *(page 38)* that decorate the **Redwork Christmas Tree** *(page 38)*. Torn fabric bows, bouquets of baby's breath, holly sprigs, and a lacy garland add a sense of sweetness. A chenille bedspread wraps the tree in snowy softness.

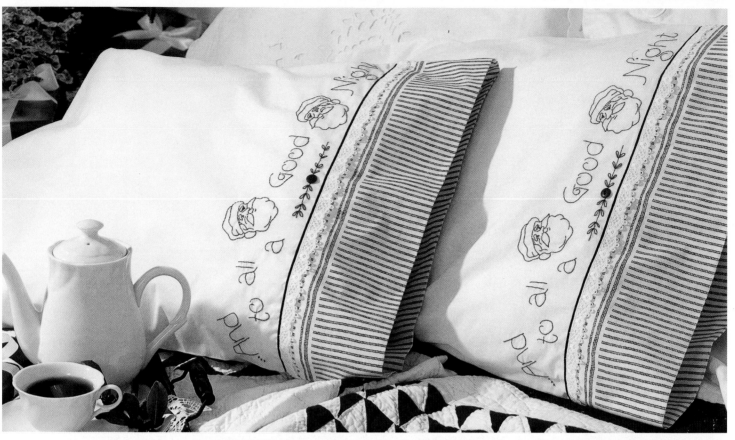

(Opposite) Designs from the pillow ornaments and lines from a classic holiday verse adorn our **Redwork Pillowcases** *(page 41)* and **"Merry Christmas" Table Topper** *(page 38)*. The projects are holiday time-savers because they're made using purchased linens. *(Above)* Stitched on muslin, the motifs also border a simple alphabet in our **Redwork Sampler** *(page 40)*, which is finished with Battenberg lace doilies.

REDWORK CHRISTMAS TREE
(Shown on page 35)

Our Redwork Christmas Tree will bring back memories of a time when your Mother or Grandmother patiently guided you in your first embroidery stitches. The pretty button-trimmed Pillow Ornaments and simple lace garland help recapture those sweet moments.

White lights twinkle cheerily through the boughs, and holly berry sprigs and bouquets of baby's breath add timeless beauty. Tied from torn fabric strips, red ticking bows make this tree a "candy cane" classic.

The tree skirt couldn't be more simple! It's a soft chenille bedspread draped around the base of the tree.

"MERRY CHRISTMAS" TABLE TOPPER
(Shown on page 36)

You will need vinegar, a red iron-on transfer pencil, tracing paper, 32" square linen table topper, embroidery hoop, red embroidery floss, sharp needle, 1/2" dia. red buttons, and 45" of 1/4"w red grosgrain ribbon.

Note: Refer to **Embroidery Stitches**, page 158, and **Stitch Key** and use two strands of floss for all embroidery stitches.

1. Mix 1 tablespoon vinegar in 8 ounces of clear water. Soak floss in mixture to release excess dye. Allow to air dry.
2. Use transfer pencil to trace the following patterns onto tracing paper: bell, page 39; bow, page 40; long border, page 41; and "Merry Christmas to all. . .," page 42. Arrange patterns on table topper. Follow pencil manufacturer's instructions to transfer three bells, two bows, and "Merry Christmas to all. . ." patterns to right side of table topper. Repeating transfer as necessary, transfer long border around table topper.
3. Place table topper in hoop. Embroider design; remove from hoop.
4. Use floss to sew one button to each corner of border. Spacing evenly along length of ribbon, tie three bows in ribbon. Tack ribbon to table topper.

PERSONALIZED STOCKINGS
(Shown on page 34)

For each stocking, you will need vinegar, tracing paper; 1/2 yd. each of red-and-white striped ticking for stocking and bleached muslin for lining; one 5" x 15" piece each of bleached muslin for cuff lining, paper-backed fusible web, and white linen for cuff (we used a piece from the border of a linen tablecloth); red iron-on transfer pencil; embroidery hoop; red embroidery floss; sharp needle; three 1/2" dia. red buttons; 15" of 3/4"w lace; and 8" of 1/4"w red grosgrain ribbon.

Note: Use a 1/4" seam allowance for all sewing. Refer to **Embroidery Stitches**, page 158, and **Stitch Key** and use two strands of floss for all embroidery stitches.

1. Mix 1 tablespoon vinegar in 8 ounces of clear water. Soak floss in mixture to release excess dye. Allow to air dry.
2. Aligning arrows and dotted lines, trace stocking top and stocking bottom patterns, page 93, onto tracing paper; cut out.
3. Matching right sides and short edges, fold fabric piece for stocking in half. Using pattern, cut stocking from fabric. Repeat using muslin for stocking lining.
4. Leaving top edge open, sew stocking pieces together. Clip curves; turn right side out. Repeat to sew lining pieces together; do not turn.
5. Fuse cuff lining to wrong side of linen. Matching short edges, fold cuff in half. Use straight pins to mark center and seam allowance. Use transfer pencil to trace letters for name from alphabet, page 43, onto tracing paper. Repeating design to extend border to 8", trace long border, page 41, onto tracing paper. Centering design between pins, arrange patterns on cuff with end of border at one short edge. Follow pencil manufacturer's instructions to transfer name and border to cuff.
6. Place cuff in hoop. Embroider design; remove from hoop. Use floss to sew buttons to cuff.
7. Topstitch lace along bottom edge of cuff. Matching right sides, sew short edges of cuff together. Matching raw edges and wrong side of cuff to right side of stocking, place cuff over stocking. Sew cuff to stocking. Press seam allowance to wrong side of stocking.
8. For hanging loop, fold ribbon in half. Tack ribbon ends to top of stocking at heel seam.

9. Press top edge of lining 1/4" to wrong side. Place lining in stocking. Hand sew pressed edge of lining to seam allowance of stocking.

PILLOW ORNAMENTS
(Shown on page 35)

For each ornament, you will need vinegar, red iron-on transfer pencil, tracing paper, two 10" squares of bleached muslin, embroidery hoop, red embroidery floss, sharp needle, four 1/2" dia. red buttons, polyester fiberfill, and two 10" lengths of 1/4"w red grosgrain ribbon.

Note: Refer to **Embroidery Stitches**, page 158, and **Stitch Key** and use two strands of floss for all embroidery stitches.

1. Mix 1 tablespoon vinegar in 8 ounces of clear water. Soak floss in mixture to release excess dye. Allow to air dry.
2. Use transfer pencil to trace desired pattern onto tracing paper. Follow pencil manufacturer's instructions to transfer pattern to center of one fabric square.
3. Place square in hoop. Embroider design; remove from hoop.
4. Sew one button to each corner of design. Matching right sides and leaving an opening for turning, sew squares together 1/2" from design. Clip corners; turn right side out.
5. Lightly stuff ornament with fiberfill. Hand sew opening closed.
6. For hanger, fold one ribbon length in half. Sew ribbon ends to back of ornament. Tie remaining ribbon length into a bow. Sew bow to front of ornament.

STITCH KEY	
Stitch Name	**Symbol**
French Knot	●
Lazy Daisy	⬯
Running Stitch	- - - -
Back Stitch	——

BELL ORNAMENT

BALL ORNAMENT

STOCKING ORNAMENT

SANTA ORNAMENT

39

REDWORK SAMPLER
(Shown on page 37)

You will need vinegar, 18" x 20" piece of paper-backed fusible web, two 18" x 20" pieces of bleached muslin, red iron-on transfer pencil, tracing paper, embroidery hoop, red embroidery floss, sharp needle, two $9^1/_2$" dia. linen doilies with Battenberg lace trim, $^1/_4$"w and $^1/_2$"w paper-backed fusible web tape, $19^1/_2$" x 21" piece of red-and-white striped ticking for backing, straight pins, two yds. of $^3/_4$"w flat lace, four $^1/_2$" dia. red buttons, 28" of $^1/_4$"w red grosgrain ribbon, $20^1/_2$" of $^1/_2$"w flat lace, and a 6" x 18" piece of bleached muslin for hanging sleeve.

Note: Refer to **Embroidery Stitches**, page 158, and **Stitch Key**, page 38, and use two strands of floss for all embroidery stitches.

1. Mix 1 tablespoon vinegar in 8 ounces of clear water. Soak floss in mixture to release excess dye. Allow to air dry.
2. Cut doilies in half; discard one piece.
3. Matching raw edges, fuse 18" x 20" muslin pieces together.

4. Use transfer pencil to trace alphabet, page 43; Santa, bell, ball, and stocking ornaments without borders, page 39; bow and leaves and bow only onto tracing paper. For borders, trace long border pattern, page 41, repeating as necessary to make two $13^1/_2$" top/bottom borders and two $15^3/_4$" side borders.
5. For sampler, arrange patterns on muslin. Follow pencil manufacturer's instructions to transfer patterns to sampler. Place sampler in hoop. Embroider designs. Remove from hoop; press. Repeat to embroider bow and leaves on one doily piece.
6. Trim edges of sampler to $^1/_4$" from border.
7. For backing, fuse web tape to wrong side of ticking along all edges; do not remove paper backing. Press edges $^1/_2$" to wrong side; unfold and remove paper backing. Refold and fuse short, then long edges in place.
8. Center sampler on right side of backing; pin in place. Using a narrow zigzag stitch, sew sampler to backing. Overlapping ends, topstitch lace around edges of sampler.

9. Sew one button at each corner of sampler. Tie a bow at center of ribbon. Sew bow to sampler; arrange streamers and tack in place
10. Fuse $^1/_4$"w web tape to wrong side of backing along bottom edge; remove paper backing. Overlapping to fit along bottom edge of backing and with stitched doily at center, arrange and fuse raw edges of doily pieces to wrong side of backing.
11. Topstitch $^1/_2$"w lace to doily pieces just below bottom edge of backing.
12. For hanging sleeve, press short edges of 6" x 18" muslin piece $^1/_4$" to wrong side twice; stitch in place. Matching right sides, sew long edges together to form tube. Turn sleeve right side out; press flat. Center one long edge of sleeve along top edge of back of sampler. Being careful not to sew through front, hand sew long edges of tube to sampler.

BOW AND LEAVES

REDWORK PILLOWCASES

(Shown on page 36)

You will need vinegar, red iron-on transfer pencil, tracing paper, pair of purchased pillowcases (we used white pillowcases with red-and-white striped trims), embroidery hoop, red embroidery floss, sharp needle, two 1/2" dia. red buttons, and two 41" lengths of 3/4"w lace.

Note: Refer to **Embroidery Stitches**, page 158, and **Stitch Key**, page 38, and use two strands of floss for all embroidery stitches.

1. Mix 1 tablespoon vinegar in 8 ounces of clear water. Soak floss in mixture to release excess dye. Allow to air dry.
2. For each pillowcase, use transfer pencil to trace two short borders and two Santa patterns, page 39, (one of each in reverse) and ". . .And to all a Good Night" onto tracing paper. Arrange patterns on pillowcase above trim. Follow pencil manufacturer's instructions to transfer patterns to pillowcase.
3. Place pillowcase in hoop. Embroider designs; remove from hoop.
4. Sew button on border. Overlapping ends at back, topstitch lace around pillowcase at inside seam of trim.

SHORT BORDER

LONG BORDER

Merry Christmas to all ...

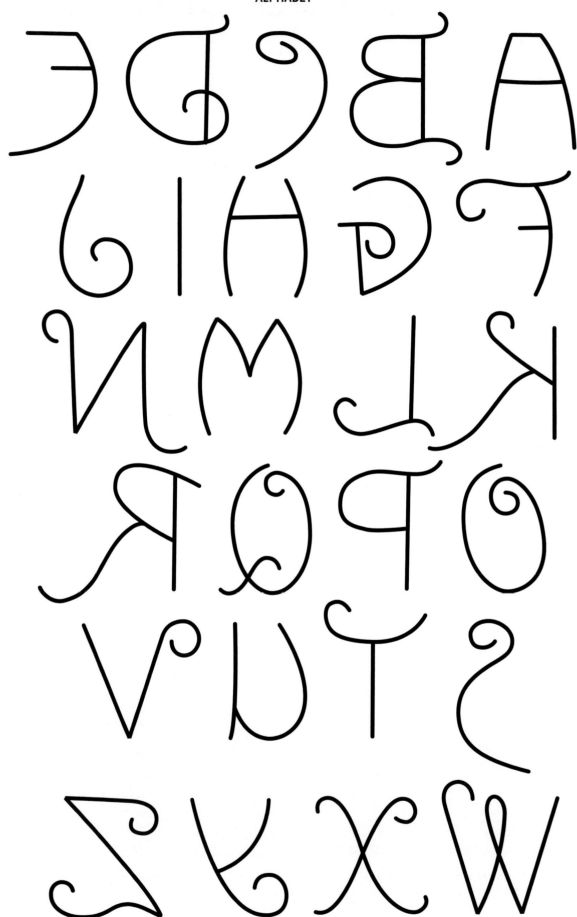

NATURE'S GLORY

*S*imple elements garnered from nature are enhanced by earth's precious metals
to create this collection of opulent accents for the home. The dazzling display, which begins
with a compelling centerpiece, abounds with nature's glory. A welcoming wreath blends grace
and beauty, and a shimmering swag showcases a prized piece of artwork. A grouping of tailored
topiaries creates a handsome vignette, and flickering candles dress the mantel in luxurious
style. Creating natural beauty has never been this easy! Instructions begin on page 48.

An artful arrangement of painted dried fruit and leaves, our **Nature's Glory Centerpiece** *(page 48)* begins with a swath
of luxurious fabric. Vintage unmatched silver candlesticks enhance the formal display, which is softened by the addition
of a **Silvery Bird Nest** *(page 48)* and a plump, sleek quail. *(Opposite)* Equally elegant, the coordinating **Bountiful Wreath**
(page 48) embraces an abundance of natural elements.

A contrast of color and texture, this **Picture Swag** *(page 48)* naturally accents a painting. Gleaming ribbons crown the piece with richness.

Moss, ferns, and pomegranates form the humble beginnings of these **Gilded Topiaries** *(page 49)*, which are displayed together to create a stately setting.

(Opposite) Elements from the collection are combined with gossamer fabric and glowing candlelight for **A Glorious Mantel** *(page 49)*. A hurricane globe filled with hazelnuts and trimmed with a silvery ribbon holds a sponge-painted pillar.

NATURE'S GLORY CENTERPIECE
(Shown on page 44)

A length of rich jacquard fabric provides the foundation for this bountiful centerpiece. The fabric flows softly across the table, drawing the viewer's eye to the treasures nestled in its folds.

To recreate this sumptuous centerpiece, fill your favorite silver bowl to the brim with nature's glory. Dried pomegranates, artichokes, and assorted leaves sprayed with Design Master® silver, gold, and copper spray paint provide a dramatic focal point for an exquisite table decoration. Accent these natural riches with pinecones, assorted nuts, and a plump 4" tall quail.

You'll set a peaceful mood for your holiday gatherings when you display our earthly wealth in all its splendor. Nearby, artificial eggs painted silver rest serenely in a purchased nest. An assortment of candlesticks offers a flicker of light to chase away the shadows.

BOUNTIFUL WREATH
(Shown on page 45)

You will need floral wire; wire cutters; 18" dia. sweet huck wreath; Design Master® silver, gold, and copper spray paint; items to decorate wreath (we used dried fern, hydrangea, salal leaves, pomegranates, mini artichokes, pinecones, assorted nuts, gold silk ivy garland, and a 4"h artificial quail); hot glue gun; one Silvery Bird Nest; and five 14" lengths each of 1"w silver mesh wired ribbon, 1½"w gold mesh ribbon, and 1¾"w copper mesh wired ribbon.

Note: Allow paint and glue to dry after each application.

1. For hanger, bend an 18" length of wire in half. Twist wire together 2" from bend to form a loop. Keeping loop at back of wreath, wrap wire ends around wreath; twist ends together to secure.
2. Paint items to decorate wreath as desired. Glue eggs in nest.
3. Using floral wire and glue, attach items to wreath.
4. Tie one each of silver, gold, and copper ribbon lengths together into a bow. Repeat to make a total of five bows. Arrange bows evenly around wreath; glue to secure.

SILVERY BIRD NEST
(Shown on page 44)

For each nest, you will need Design Master® silver spray paint, two artificial eggs, hot glue gun, and an artificial nest.

1. Spray eggs silver; allow to dry.
2. Arrange and glue eggs in nest.

PICTURE SWAG
(Shown on page 46)

You will need Design Master® silver, gold, and copper spray paint; assorted items to decorate swag (we used dried fern, hydrangea, salal leaves, a pomegranate, mini artichokes, pinecones, brazil nuts, and gold silk ivy); floral wire; wire cutters; 32" twig swag; hot glue gun; and 42" each of 1"w silver mesh wired ribbon, 1½"w gold mesh ribbon, and 1¾"w copper mesh wired ribbon.

Note: Allow paint and glue to dry after each application.

1. Paint items to decorate swag as desired.
2. Using floral wire and glue, attach items to swag.
3. Tie ribbon lengths together into a bow; glue to top of swag.

GILDED TOPIARIES (Shown on page 46)

POMEGRANATE TOPIARY
You will need an 18"h twig topiary form, 18" of $1/2$" dia. dowel rod, floral foam, 4 yds. of gold cord, 52" of 1"w silver mesh wired ribbon, floral wire, wire cutters, Design Master® copper spray paint, dried pomegranates, 10" dia. lichen-covered wreath, sheet moss, 12" dia. urn, and a hot glue gun.

Note: Allow paint and glue to dry after each application.

1. Paint pomegranates.
2. Trimming to fit, fill urn with floral foam. Glue wreath to foam. Insert dowel into foam. Fill center of wreath with sheet moss. Glue pomegranates around wreath.
3. Place topiary form over dowel. Spot gluing to secure, wrap cord around topiary.
4. Follow **Making a Bow**, page 156, to make a bow with four 7" loops and two 12" streamers. Glue bow to topiary.

MOSS TOPIARY
You will need Design Master® silver spray paint, two dried salal leaves, 6" dia. pot, floral foam, hot glue gun, sheet moss, 22"h moss topiary form with trunk, 4 yds. of silver cord, and 1 yd. of gold cord.

Note: Allow paint and glue to dry after each application.

1. Paint leaves.
2. Trimming to fit, fill pot with floral foam. Glue moss over top of foam. Insert trunk of topiary into foam.
3. Spot gluing to secure, wind 3 yds. of silver cord around topiary from top to bottom, then bottom to top.
4. Tie gold and remaining silver cords together into a bow; knot cord ends. Glue bow and leaves to top of topiary.

FERN TOPIARY
You will need Design Master® silver spray paint, dried salal leaves, 12" dia. wire urn, sheet moss, floral foam, hot glue gun, two 26" lengths of $1/2$" dia. dowel rod, $2 1/2$ yds. of $1 3/4$"w copper mesh wired ribbon, and a 26"h vine-wrapped fern topiary form.

Note: Allow paint and glue to dry after each application.

1. Paint leaves.
2. Line urn with sheet moss. Trimming to fit, fill urn with floral foam. Glue moss over top of foam. Insert dowel rods into foam.
3. Insert leaves under vine on topiary form; glue to secure. Gluing ends to secure, wrap ribbon around topiary. Place topiary over dowels.

A GLORIOUS MANTEL
(Shown on page 47)

Glimmering tulle spills over the edge of this mantelpiece and reflects the light from this shining collection. Stacks of leather-bound books complement the gilded fruit, glittering bead garland, and Silvery Bird Nest. A hurricane lamp plays host to dried naturals as it sports a glistening ribbon. An assortment of candlesticks spreads the radiance.

Keeping this little slice of heaven firmly on earth, twig balls and Gilded Topiaries remind us of the simple beauty of nature.

Santa, Look At This!

Christmas is the perfect time to encourage children to be creative, and this collection, designed especially for kids, makes it easy for them to be proud of their accomplishments. With just a little help from a grown-up, youngsters can craft a variety of quick-and-easy projects, from coffee filter angels and cowbell reindeer to painted handprint sweatshirts or a felt stocking. Whether the projects are fashioned at home or at school, children will be having fun, developing skills, and learning that "I can do it!" Instructions begin on page 54.

These cute projects encourage "hands on" experience! There are two **Handprint Sweatshirts** *(page 55)* — the Santa is simply a trio of painted palm prints finished with fingerprint eyes and pom-poms. A cluster of palm prints form the Christmas tree, which is trimmed with a garland of dimensional paint and jewel stones. *(Opposite, inset)* Youngsters can create our **Handprint Santa Ornament** *(page 54)* from a plain papier-mâché ball. For a fun finish, thumbprints were used in the "Ho Ho Ho," and pinky finger prints lot Santa's eyes.

51

(Clockwise from top left) Holiday shapes cut from craft foam deck a painted **Message Chalkboard** *(page 57)* with cheer. Dressed in a black felt top hat, our **Peppermint Stick Man** *(page 57)* is a festive fashion star. The lacy **Paper Bag Angel** *(page 56)* is simply a plain white lunch sack embellished with paper doilies and a poster board head. Made from a "recycled" baby food container, our **Santa Candy Jar** *(page 56)* is a sweet little keepsake or gift. The **Pinecone Santas** *(page 56)* are natural tree trimmers, especially when peppermint candies are added for color.

(Clockwise from top left) Kids can create a dozen **Cookie Cutter Ornaments** *(page 55)* like our candy cane and Christmas tree in no time at all. **Coffee Filter Angel Ornaments** *(page 57)* are great little projects for preschool or Sunday school classes. Fashioned from felt, our **Pom-Pom Snowman Stocking** *(page 55)* features a snowman juggling "snowballs." The main things needed to build **Sock Snowman Ornaments** *(page 54)* are some socks, buttons, and a jingle bell. Freehand drawings add charm to a **Photo Frame Ornament** *(page 54)*, which gets its shine from aluminum foil. Ring in the holidays with our whimsical **Cowbell Reindeer** *(page 56)*. He's quick to make with just a few trims.

PHOTO FRAME ORNAMENT
(Shown on page 53)

You will need two 4" x 5" pieces of craft foam, two 6" x 7" pieces of aluminum foil, low-temperature glue gun, photo to fit 2" x 3" opening, 9" of silver tinsel stem, black fine-point marker, and four 7mm red acrylic jewels.

Note: Adult supervision required.

1. Cut a 2" x 3" opening in center of one foam piece for frame front.
2. For frame front and frame back, center foam piece on dull side of foil. Fold corners of foil diagonally over corners of foam; glue in place. Fold edges of foil over edges of foam; glue in place. Refer to **Fig. 1** to cut foil in frame front opening 1" from edges of opening. Fold flaps of foil over edges of opening; glue to secure.

Fig. 1

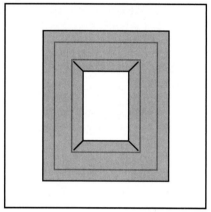

3. Center and glue photo in opening of frame front. Glue frame front and frame back together.
4. For hanger, insert ends of tinsel stem through top corners of frame; bend and twist to secure.
5. Have child draw designs around edge of frame with marker (we drew hearts, snowflakes, and trees).
6. Glue jewels to front of frame.

SNOWMAN SOCK ORNAMENT
(Shown on page 53)

You will need utility scissors, a craft stick, orange acrylic paint, paintbrush, 3" dia. plastic foam ball, one white and one red child-size sock, rubber band, craft glue, 10" of 1/8"w green ribbon, 1/2" dia. jingle bell, red thread, two 1/2" dia. black shank buttons for eyes, and assorted buttons for mouth.

Note: Adult supervision required.

1. For nose, use utility scissors to cut a 2" length from craft stick. Cut each end of stick at an angle. Paint nose orange; allow to dry.
2. For head, place ball in toe of white sock. Gather sock at top of ball; secure with rubber band. Cut off cuff above rubber band.
3. For hat, fold cuff of red sock up 1". Place hat on head over gathers; glue to secure. Tie ribbon into a bow through eye of bell. Sew bell to tip of hat.
4. Glue buttons to head for eyes and mouth. Insert nose in head.

HANDPRINT SANTA ORNAMENT
(Shown on page 51)

You will need white, flesh, red, and brown acrylic paint; paintbrushes; 4" dia. papier-mâché ornament with hanger; black permanent medium-point marker; two 1/2" dia. white pom-poms; 3/8" dia. red wooden bead; and craft glue.

Note: Adult supervision required.

1. For each stamp, refer to **Fig. 1** to apply paint to child's hand. With fingers together, stamp hand on two sides of ornament; allow to dry.

Fig. 1

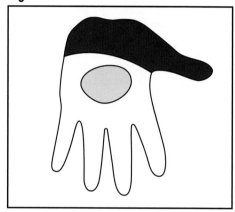

2. For eyes, apply brown paint to tip of child's smallest finger. Stamp eyes on Santa faces; allow to dry. Apply brown paint to tip of child's thumb. Leaving spaces for "H's", stamp three thumbprints above each Santa; allow to dry.
3. Use marker to draw "H's" and dots. Glue pom-poms to Santa hats; allow to dry. Thread hanger through bead; glue bead to ball and allow to dry.

COOKIE CUTTER ORNAMENTS

(Shown on page 53)

Note: Adult supervision required.

CANDY CANE
You will need one 5" x 8" piece each of paper-backed fusible web, red-and-white striped fabric, and cardboard; 6"h candy cane cookie cutter; craft glue; eight 7mm red acrylic jewels; assorted white and red buttons; and 6" of gold cord.

1. Fuse web to wrong side of fabric. Remove paper backing; fuse fabric to cardboard.
2. Draw around cookie cutter on fused cardboard; cut out along drawn line.
3. Arrange and glue jewels and buttons on candy cane; allow to dry.
4. For hanger, glue ends of cord to back of ornament; allow to dry.

CHRISTMAS TREE
For each ornament, you will need one 5" x 7" piece each of paper-backed fusible web, green fabric, and cardboard; 5 1/2"h tree cookie cutter; craft glue; red baby rickrack; one 1/2"w gold star acrylic jewel; assorted gold and red acrylic jewels; and 6" of gold cord.

1. Fuse web to wrong side of fabric. Remove paper backing; fuse fabric to cardboard.
2. Draw around cookie cutter on fused cardboard; cut out along drawn line.
3. Glue rickrack and jewels on tree; allow to dry.
4. For hanger, glue ends of cord to back of ornament; allow to dry.

HANDPRINT SWEATSHIRTS

(Shown on page 50)

Note: Adult supervision required.

TREE SWEATSHIRT
You will need a child-size white sweatshirt; green and brown acrylic paint; freezer-paper or T-shirt form; paintbrush; gold dimensional fabric paint; 16mm gold, red, and blue acrylic jewels; and a 20mm gold acrylic jewel.

1. Refer to **Painting Techniques**, page 157, to prepare sweatshirt.
2. Use brown paint to paint a 23"h tree trunk above center of waistband; allow to dry.
3. For each stamp, paint child's hand green. Beginning at bottom, stamp handprints in rows to form tree shape; allow to dry.
4. Use dimensional paint to paint garland. To attach each jewel, squeeze a dot of dimensional paint slightly smaller than jewel onto sweatshirt. Press jewel into paint; allow to dry.
5. Use dimensional paint to draw snowflakes on sweatshirt. Dot dimensional paint over tree and front of sweatshirt; allow to dry.

SANTA SWEATSHIRT
You will need a child-size grey sweatshirt; white, flesh, red, and brown acrylic paint; freezer paper or T-shirt form; paintbrush; fabric glue; and three 1/2" dia. white pom-poms.

1. Refer to **Painting Techniques**, page 157, to prepare sweatshirt.
2. For each stamp, refer to **Fig. 1** of Handprint Santa Ornament to apply paint to child's hand. Stamp hand three times across front of sweatshirt; allow to dry.
3. For eyes, apply brown paint to tip of child's smallest finger. Stamp eyes on Santa faces; allow to dry. Glue one pom-pom to each Santa hat; allow to dry.

POM-POM SNOWMAN STOCKING

(Shown on page 53)

You will need tracing paper; two 10" x 13" pieces of red felt; white and black sport weight yarn; large-eye needle; craft glue; two 1" dia., nine 3/8" dia., and four 3/4" dia. white pom-poms; and two 3mm black pom-poms for eyes.

Note: Adult supervision required.

1. Aligning dotted lines and arrows, trace stocking top A and stocking bottom onto tracing paper; cut out. Using pattern, cut two stocking pieces from felt.
2. Use white yarn to work **Running Stitches**, page 159, to outline heel and toe areas on front of stocking.
3. Matching wrong sides, place stocking front and back together. Leaving top open, use white yarn to work **Overcast Stitches**, page 159, along edges of stocking to sew stocking pieces together.
4. For mouth, tie two knots 3/4" apart in a length of black yarn; trim ends close to knots. Glue eyes and mouth to one 3/4" dia. pom-pom. For arms, knot ends of a 3" length of black yarn; trim ends close to knots.
5. For snowman, glue arms, head, and 1" dia. pom-poms on stocking; allow to dry. For snowballs, glue six 3/8" dia. pom-poms in an arch above head.
6. Glue remaining pom-poms along top edge of stocking. Tie 21" of black yarn into a bow. Glue bow to corner of stocking; allow to dry.

STOCKING BOTTOM

STOCKING TOP B

STOCKING TOP A

PAPER BAG ANGEL

(Shown on page 52)

For each angel, you will need a lunch-size white paper bag, craft glue, two 8" dia. paper doilies, transparent tape, tracing paper, poster board, black permanent fine-point marker, pink colored pencil, natural raffia, 1/8"w gold ribbon, and an 18mm star sequin.

Note: Adult supervision required. Allow glue to dry after each application.

1. Fold top corners of bag to back to form point; glue to secure.
2. For dress, wrap one doily around point of bag; glue edges of doily to back of bag. For wings, gather center of remaining doily; tape to secure. Glue wings to back of bag.
3. Trace head pattern onto tracing paper; cut out. Using pattern, cut head from poster board. Use marker and colored pencil to draw face. For hair, glue 5 1/2" lengths of raffia around face. For halo, form a 5" length of ribbon into a circle; glue ends to back of head.
4. Glue head to bag. Tie a 7" length of ribbon into a bow. Glue bow and sequin at neck.

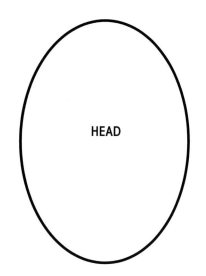

HEAD

COWBELL REINDEER

(Shown on page 53)

You will need a low-temperature glue gun, 20mm oval wiggle eyes, 1" dia. brown pom-pom for nose, 3"h cowbell, black permanent medium-point marker, 4" lengths of natural raffia, two 12" brown chenille stems, and 12" of 3/4"w red polka-dot ribbon.

Note: Adult supervision required.

1. Glue eyes and nose to one side of bell. Use marker to draw mouth and eyebrows. For hair, fold raffia in half; glue to top of bell.
2. For antlers, cut each stem into 5" and 7" lengths. Twist one end of each 7" length around handle. Twist one 5" length around each 7" length; shape antlers. Tie ribbon into a bow around handle.

SANTA CANDY JAR

(Shown on page 52)

You will need tracing paper; tape; large baby food jar with lid; white, red, and black acrylic paint; paintbrushes; black permanent medium-point marker; flesh-colored candy; green yarn; 3/4" dia. white button; low-temperature glue gun; and a child-size red sock.

Note: Adult supervision required. Allow paint to dry after each application.

1. Trace Santa pattern onto tracing paper. Tape pattern inside jar. Use white paint to paint eyebrows, mustache, and area below mustache for beard. Use red paint to paint nose and mouth. Use marker to color eyes and outline mustache and eyebrows. Remove pattern. Fill jar with candy; place lid on jar.
2. For hat, thread 6" of yarn through button; tie into a bow. Glue button to toe of sock. Fold cuff of sock 3/4" to right side. Place hat on jar.

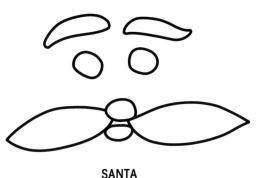

SANTA

PINECONE SANTAS

(Shown on page 52)

Note: Adult supervision required.

PEPPERMINT SANTA

For each ornament, you will need a 3"h plastic foam egg, flesh-colored acrylic paint, paintbrush, two straight pins with black heads, low-temperature glue gun, one 5mm red pom-pom, polyester fiberfill, child-size red sock, thread, one 3/4" dia. white pom-pom, straight pins with red heads, large pinecone with flat bottom, and wrapped round peppermint candies.

1. For head, paint egg flesh; allow to dry. Insert black pins into head for eyes. Glue red pom-pom to head for nose. Arrange and glue fiberfill on head for hair, beard, and mustache.
2. For hat, cut cuff from sock; discard toe. Knot thread around cut edge of cuff to gather. Glue white pom-pom to gathered end. Fold cuff of hat 1/2" to right side twice. Place hat on head; secure with pins between cuff and hat.
3. Glue head to pinecone. Insert candies in pinecone.

HANGING ORNAMENT

For each ornament, you will need flesh-colored acrylic paint, paintbrush, 2"h plastic foam egg, two straight pins with black heads, low-temperature glue gun, 5mm red pom-pom, polyester fiberfill, child-size red sock, thread, 3/4" dia. white pom-pom, straight pins with red heads, 6" narrow pinecone, and 12" of 1/4"w red satin ribbon.

1. For head, paint egg flesh; allow to dry. Insert black pins into head for eyes. Glue red pom-pom to head for nose. Arrange and glue fiberfill on head for hair, beard, and mustache.
2. For hat, cut cuff from sock; discard toe. Knot thread around cut edge of cuff to gather. Glue white pom-pom to gathered end. Fold cuff of hat 1/2" to right side twice. Place hat on head; secure with pins.
3. Glue head to pinecone. Pin ribbon ends to back of head for hanger.

MESSAGE CHALKBOARD
(Shown on page 52)

You will need white and red acrylic paint; paintbrush; 6½" x 8½" chalkboard with wooden frame; tracing paper; white, yellow, red, blue, and green craft foam; black permanent fine-point marker; ¼" dia. hole punch; low-temperature glue gun; 13" of ⅝"w green grosgrain ribbon; 15" of 1"w red striped grosgrain ribbon; and chalk.

Note: Adult supervision required.

1. Paint chalkboard frame white; allow to dry. Paint red stripes along short ends of frame; allow to dry.
2. Trace tree, star, stocking, and cuff patterns onto tracing paper; cut out. Using patterns, cut shapes from craft foam. Use marker to draw "stitches" along edges of foam pieces and each white area on frame.
3. For ornaments on tree, punch holes from assorted colors of craft foam. Glue ornaments to tree. Glue cuff to stocking. Glue shapes to frame.
4. For hanger, glue one end of green ribbon to each top back corner of frame. Tie striped ribbon into a bow around hanger.
5. Use chalk to write message on chalkboard.

COFFEE FILTER ANGEL ORNAMENT
(Shown on page 53)

You will need two coffee filters, craft glue, flesh colored pencil, drawing compass, poster board, black permanent fine-point marker, curly doll hair, gold tinsel stem, assorted buttons, and white embroidery floss.

Note: Adult supervision required. Allow glue to dry after each application.

1. For dress, fold one filter in half. Overlap folded edges to make a cone shape; glue to secure. With glued edges at back, flatten cone.
2. For wings, cut remaining filter in half. Fold each piece in half; fold in half again. Glue wings to back of dress.
3. For head, use compass to draw a 1½" dia. circle on poster board; cut out. Use pencil to color circle. Use marker to draw eyes and mouth. Glue doll hair to head. For halo, twist ends of a 3½" length of chenille stem together to form a circle; glue to head.
4. Glue head and buttons to dress. For hanger, glue ends of a 7" length of floss to back of head.

PEPPERMINT STICK MAN
(Shown on page 52)

You will need white, yellow, and red acrylic paint; paintbrush; jumbo craft stick; two 1½"w wooden stars; 1"w wooden heart; black permanent fine-point marker; tracing paper, black felt; low-temperature glue gun; 1" dia. wrapped peppermint candy stick, red and green chenille stems; and two ¾" dia. wiggle eyes.

Note: For decorative purposes only. Adult supervision required. Allow paint and glue to dry after each application.

1. Paint craft stick white, stars yellow, and heart red. Use tip of paintbrush handle to add white dots to heart.
2. Use marker to draw "stitches" along edges of stars.
3. Trace hat, hat brim, and hat top patterns onto tracing paper; cut out. Using patterns, cut hat pieces from felt. Glue hat top to one end of candy stick. Overlapping ends, glue hat around same end of candy stick. Place hat brim on candy stick; glue to bottom edge of crown. Glue 4" of green chenille stem around hat for hat trim.
4. Glue eyes to a 1½" length of red chenille stem. For mouth, bend 2½" of red chenille stem into a "U" shape. Glue stem ends to back of eyes. Glue face to candy stick.
5. For arms, glue stars to each end of craft stick. Glue arms to back and heart to front of candy stick.

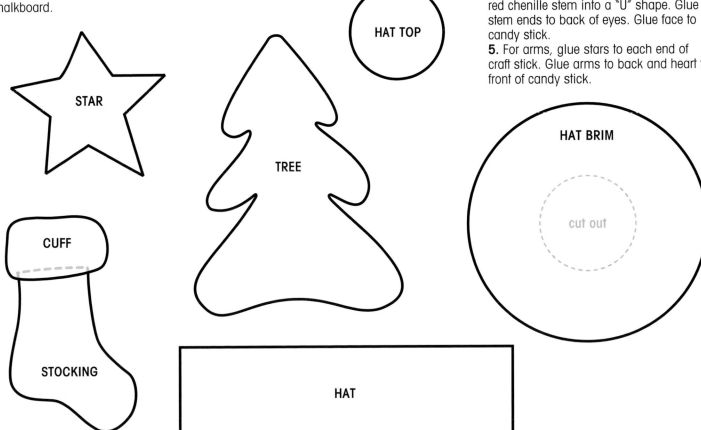

STAR

HAT TOP

TREE

CUFF

HAT BRIM

cut out

STOCKING

HAT

KEEP CHRISTMAS IN YOUR HEART

Hearts abound in this collection, which gets its cheery look from a palette of vibrant color. Trimmed in a garland of white picket fences, the fun, folksy tree plays host to a multitude of winsome ornaments — from painted canvas characters and fabric-covered hearts to festive stars. And of course, we've included an angel to top the tree! Heartwarming messages embellish our framed tree trimmers, photo album cover, and greeting cards, and a photo frame reminds us that family is at the heart of Christmas. You'll also find some great ideas for decorating gift bags, furniture, and more. Instructions begin on page 64.

Keep holiday memories close at hand with this festive **Appliquéd Photo Album** *(page 64)*. Embroidered using simple running stitches, the sentimental message is enhanced by a homey scene.

Love is at the center of our **Keep Christmas in Your Heart Tree** *(page 64)*, which heralds the season in a series of **Heartfelt Framed Messages** *(page 66)*, **Puffed Heart Ornaments** *(page 64)*, and **Cardboard and Fabric Heart Ornaments** *(page 70)*. Foam **Star Ornaments** *(page 67)* and "tapers" fashioned from clip-on lights and sheets of beeswax add to the brilliance of the tree, and painted **Canvas Characters** *(page 68)* include angels, snowmen, and Santas. *(Opposite)* A star-studded frame showcases our **Angel Tree Topper** *(page 68)*, and our **Starry Heart Frame** *(page 66)* recognizes the importance of family. The collection wraps up with a selection of easy-to-assemble **Homey Gift Bags** *(page 69)*.

Our **Santa Picket** *(page 70)* does a stand-up job of spreading Christmas cheer. A wooden heart shows his kind, gentle spirit. *(Opposite)* These easy-to-fashion **Christmas Cards** *(page 67)* will leave you plenty of time to shop for the perfect gift! Designed to nurture your creative possibilities, our **Happy Heart Chairs** *(page 69)* reflect the collection's lively color scheme.

KEEP CHRISTMAS IN YOUR HEART TREE

(Shown on page 59)

You'll have a fun and folksy Christmas when this lovable country tree sets the theme. The 7½-foot weeping mountain pine looks anything but sad! It's bedecked with happy hearts from its angel-topped tip to its plaid fabric-skirted bottom.

Star Ornaments hang here and there, while stuffed Canvas Characters (page 68) help spread seasonal cheer. These fun-loving Santas, angels, and snowmen add a playful touch. For the Angel Tree Topper (page 68) one of the angel characters keeps a watchful eye over the festivities from a crafty frame.

Heartfelt Framed Messages (page 66) are friendly reminders of the spirit of Christmas. Cardboard and Fabric Heart Ornaments (page 70) and Puffed Heart Ornaments further brighten the boughs and help make your heart merry.

Glowing "tapers" are a snap to make by wrapping sheets of honeycomb beeswax around clip-on candle light strings.

Adding whimsy and a familiar touch of yesteryear, purchased garlands of picket fences and popcorn wind through the branches.

PUFFED HEART ORNAMENTS

(Shown on page 60)

For each ornament, you will need tracing paper, corrugated cardboard, red acrylic paint, paintbrush, 12" shoestring, wood-tone spray, hot glue gun, 3"w puffed wooden heart, ³/₄" dia. red button, and a hole punch.

Note: Allow paint and wood-tone spray to dry after each application.

1. Trace heart F, page 71, onto tracing paper; cut out. Using pattern, cut heart from cardboard. Paint corrugated side of cardboard heart red. Spray shoestring with wood-tone spray.
2. Center and glue wooden heart on cardboard heart. Glue button to wooden heart. For handle, punch two holes at top of cardboard heart. Thread ends of shoestring through holes; knot ends at front.

APPLIQUÉD PHOTO ALBUM (Shown on page 58)

You will need an 11" x 13" photo album with center rings; fabric to cover album; hot glue gun; poster board; fabric to line album; paper-backed fusible web; green print fabric for bow; pinking shears; one yd. of 1"w red grosgrain ribbon; hot glue gun, fabric marking pencil, 9½" x 11½" piece of green felt; yellow, red, green, brown, and black print fabrics for appliqués; tracing paper; transfer paper; yellow, red, and black embroidery floss; decorative-edge craft scissors; and lightweight corrugated cardboard.

Note: Follow **Embroidery Stitches**, page 158, and use six strands of floss for all embroidery stitches.

1. To cover album, draw around open album on wrong side of fabric. Cut out fabric 2" outside drawn line.
2. Center open album on wrong side of fabric piece. Fold corners of fabric diagonally over corners of album; glue in place. Fold edges of fabric over edges of cover, trimming fabric to fit under album hardware; glue in place.
3. To line inside of album, cut two pieces of poster board 1" smaller than front of album. Cut two pieces of fabric 2" larger than poster board pieces.
4. Center one poster board piece on one side of one fabric piece. Fold corners of fabric piece diagonally over corners of poster board; glue in place. Fold edges of fabric over edges of poster board; glue in place. Repeat with remaining poster board and fabric.
5. Glue covered poster board to inside covers.

6. For bow, fuse web to wrong side of green fabric. Use pinking shears to cut a ³/₄" x 1 yd.-length of green fabric. Center and fuse strip to ribbon; cut ribbon in half. Glue one end of each ribbon to outside opening edge of front and back covers.
7. Use fabric marking pencil and refer to album sections diagram to mark sections on felt piece.
8. Using fabrics for appliqués and patterns, pages 65 and 71, follow **Making Appliqués**, page 156, to make one each of heart A, heart L, tree trunk, ³/₄" x 1¹/₄" door, ³/₄" square chimney, roof, roof side, 2½" x 3⅝" house front, 1½" x 2½" house side, and 1" x 6½" checkerboard base; three each of heart M and heart C appliqués; and five ³/₄" square windows and thirteen ¹/₂" square red checkerboard appliqués. Arrange and fuse appliqués to felt.
9. Trace "All Hearts Come Home For Christmas", page 65, onto tracing paper. Using transfer paper, transfer words to felt. Using red floss, work Running Stitches and Cross Stitches along section lines. Using yellow floss, work Running Stitches over words. Using black floss, work Running Stitches to outline appliqués and words and to make chimney smoke.
10. Use craft scissors to cut a 10¹/₄" x 12¹/₂" piece of cardboard. Fuse web to back of felt. Fuse felt to cardboard. Glue cardboard to front of album.

DIAGRAM

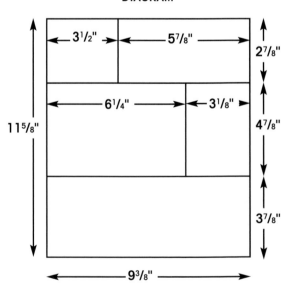

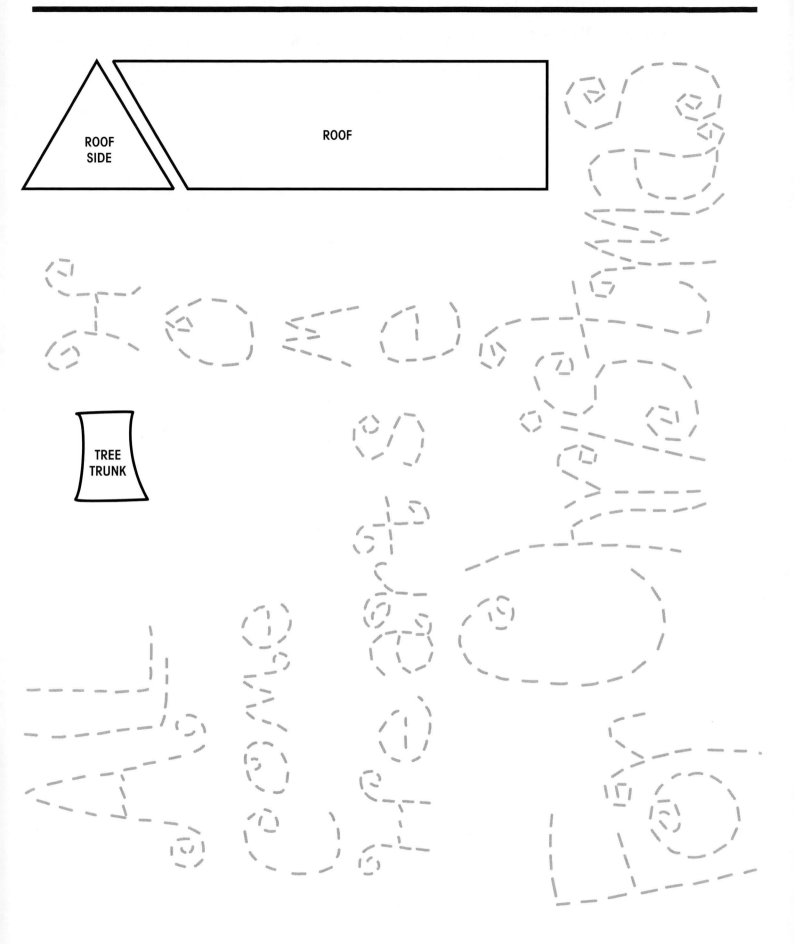

ROOF SIDE

ROOF

TREE TRUNK

65

"KEEP CHRISTMAS" FRAMED MESSAGE

You will need foam core board; craft knife; cutting mat; tracing paper; ultra-thin craft steel; decorative-edge craft scissors; paper crimping tool; red, light green, green, and beige acrylic paint; paintbrush; hot glue gun; crackle medium; clear acrylic spray sealer; black permanent fine-point marker; transfer paper; white card stock; red colored pencil; black permanent medium-point marker; and 10" of 20-gauge black craft wire.

Note: Use craft knife to cut foam core board. Allow paint, crackle medium, and sealer to dry after each application.

1. For back of frame, cut a 5" x 6" piece from foam core board. For front of frame, cut a 4" x 5" piece from foam core board with a 3" x 4" opening.
2. Trace heart J and heart K, page 71, onto tracing paper; cut out. Using patterns, cut one heart K from foam core board and one heart J from steel.
3. Use craft scissors to cut a 4$\frac{1}{2}$" x 5$\frac{1}{2}$" piece from steel. Use crimping tool to corrugate steel pieces. Paint foam core board heart red. Glue steel heart to foam core board heart.
4. Paint back of frame green. Follow manufacturer's instructions to apply crackle medium to back of frame. Paint back of frame beige. Apply sealer to back of frame. Alternating red and light green, paint stripes on front of frame. Use fine-point marker to draw lines between stripes.
5. Trace design onto tracing paper. Use transfer paper to transfer design onto card stock. Use colored pencil to color heart. Use medium-point marker to draw over message and heart. Trim design to 3$\frac{3}{4}$" x 4$\frac{3}{4}$".
6. Center and glue steel rectangle on back of frame, card stock on steel, and frame on card stock.
7. For hanger, centering foam core board heart on wire, thread wire through heart. Bend wire into a "U" shape. Apply glue to ends of wire. Insert ends into top of frame.

"SHARING" FRAMED MESSAGE

You will need foam core board, craft knife, cutting mat, tracing paper, ultra-thin craft steel, paper crimping tool, red and light green acrylic paint, paintbrush, crackle medium, clear acrylic spray sealer, transfer paper, white card stock, red colored pencil, hot glue gun, and 9" of 20-gauge black craft wire.

Note: Use craft knife to cut foam core board. Allow paint, crackle medium, and sealer to dry after each application.

1. For frame, cut a 5" square from foam core board with a 4" x 4" opening. Trace heart J and heart K, page 71, onto tracing paper; cut out. Using heart K pattern, cut four hearts from foam core board. Using heart J pattern, cut four hearts from steel. Use crimping tool to corrugate steel hearts.
2. Paint frame and foam core board hearts red. Follow manufacturer's instructions to apply crackle medium to frame. Paint frame light green. Apply sealer to frame.
3. Trace design onto tracing paper. Use transfer paper to transfer design onto card stock. Use colored pencil to color heart. Use medium-point marker to draw over message and heart. Trim design to 4$\frac{1}{2}$" square.
4. Center and glue frame over design. Glue steel hearts to foam core board hearts. Glue hearts to corners of frame.
5. For hanger, wrap center of wire around a pencil. Bend wire into a "U" shape. Apply glue to ends of wire; insert ends into top of frame.

"HOME IS WHERE..." FRAMED MESSAGE

You will need foam core board; craft knife; cutting mat; tracing paper; red, green, and beige acrylic paint; paintbrush; crackle medium; black permanent medium-point marker; clear acrylic spray sealer; 5" of 20-gauge black craft wire; green raffia; hot glue gun; paper crimping tool; and ultra-thin craft steel.

Note: Use craft knife to cut foam core board. Allow paint, crackle medium, and sealer to dry after each application.

1. For front of frame, cut a 5" square from foam core board with a 3" square opening. For border, cut a 4" square from foam core board with a 3" square opening.
2. Trace heart N, page 71, onto tracing paper; cut out. Using pattern, cut heart from foam core board.
3. Paint border and heart beige. Paint front of frame green. Follow manufacturer's instructions to apply crackle medium to base and heart. Paint front of frame and heart red.
4. Use marker to write "Home is where you hang your heart" around border. Apply sealer to foam pieces.
5. Shape one end of wire into a heart. Insert straight end through top of front of frame and into top of heart. Tie raffia into a bow. Glue bow to heart. Glue border to front of frame.
6. Use crimping tool to corrugate a piece of steel large enough to cover opening in front of frame. Glue steel to back of base.

STARRY HEART FRAME

(Shown on page 61)

You will need gold, red, and green acrylic paint; paintbrushes; 11$\frac{1}{4}$" square wooden frame; three 1$\frac{1}{2}$"w and four 1$\frac{7}{8}$"w wooden stars; crackle medium; clear acrylic spray sealer; tracing paper; decorative-edge craft scissors; ultra-thin craft steel; paper crimping tool; transfer paper; white card stock; red colored pencil; hot glue gun; 3$\frac{1}{2}$"w wooden heart; two $\frac{3}{4}$" x 10" and two $\frac{3}{4}$" x 8$\frac{1}{2}$" strips of green corrugated paper; assorted white buttons; and wood-tone spray.

Note: Allow paint, crackle medium, sealer, and wood-tone spray to dry after each application.

1. Paint frame green and stars gold. Follow manufacturer's instructions to apply crackle medium to frame. Paint front of frame red. Apply sealer to frame.
2. Trace heart D and heart E, page 71, onto tracing paper; cut out. Using heart E pattern and craft scissors, cut heart from steel. Use crimping tool to corrugate steel heart.
3. Trace design onto tracing paper. Use transfer paper to transfer design onto card stock. Use colored pencil to color heart in design. Use medium-point marker to draw over message and heart. Using heart D pattern cut design from card stock.
4. Center and glue card stock heart on wooden heart. Glue wooden heart on steel heart.
5. Glue paper strips to frame. Lightly spray stars and buttons with wood-tone. Glue steel heart to top of frame. Arrange and glue stars and buttons on frame.

CHRISTMAS CARDS (Shown on page 62)

"KEEP CHRISTMAS" CARD

You will need a 7" x 10" piece of red card stock, 5 1/4" x 7 1/4" natural-colored envelope, paper-backed fusible web, red and green print fabric, paper crimping tool, ultra-thin craft steel, tracing paper, transfer paper, white card stock, red colored pencil, black permanent medium-point and fine-point markers, hot glue gun, sewing thread, and assorted buttons.

Note: If mailing card, envelope should be marked "HAND CANCEL."

1. For card, match short edges to fold red card stock in half. Draw around flap of envelope and front of card on paper side of web. Fuse web to wrong side of fabric. Cut out flap along drawn line and card fabric 1/4" inside drawn lines. Fuse fabric to outside of envelope flap.
2. Use crimping tool to corrugate steel. Cut steel 1/2" smaller on all sides than card fabric.
3. Trace design onto tracing paper. Use transfer paper to transfer design onto card stock. Use colored pencil to color heart. Use medium-point marker to draw over message and heart. Trim design to 3"h x 4"w. Use fine-point marker to add a dot in each corner and a wavy line between each dot.
4. Center and glue message on steel. Center and glue steel on fabric. Wrap thread through holes in buttons and knot at back to secure. Glue a button to steel at each side of message.

"SHARING" CARD

You will need a 3" x 7 1/4" and a 7" x 10" piece of red card stock, 5 1/4" x 7 1/4" natural-colored envelope, hot glue gun, tracing paper, transfer paper, white card stock, red colored pencil, black permanent medium-point and fine-point markers, green corrugated paper, buttons, and green raffia.

Note: If mailing card, envelope should be marked "HAND CANCEL."

1. For card, match short edges to fold 7" x 10" piece of card stock in half. Draw around flap of envelope on remaining piece of red card stock. Cut out flap along drawn line. Glue card stock flap to outside of envelope flap.
2. Trace design onto tracing paper. Use transfer paper to transfer design onto card stock. Use colored pencil to color heart. Use medium-point marker to draw over message and heart. Trim design to 3"h x 5"w. Use fine-point marker to add a dot in each corner and a wavy line between each dot.
3. For card, cut two 1/2" x 4 1/2" and two 1/2" x 6 1/2" strips from corrugated paper; glue to card. For envelope flap, measure edges of flap; cut strips 1/2"w by the determined measurements. Glue strips to flap.
4. Glue buttons to corners of card and flap. Tie raffia into a bow. Glue bow to card.

STAR ORNAMENTS
(Shown on page 60)

For each ornament, you will need tracing paper, craft knife, cutting mat, foam core board, gold acrylic paint, paintbrush, wood-tone spray, hot glue gun, 3/4" dia. green button, and a 6" length of floral wire.

Note: Allow paint and wood-tone spray to dry after each application.

1. Trace star C, page 70, onto tracing paper; cut out. Using pattern and craft knife, cut star from foam core board.
2. Paint star gold. Spray star with wood-tone. Glue button to star. For hanger, glue one end of wire to back of star. Bend opposite end to form hook.

ANGEL TREE TOPPER
(Shown on page 61)

You will need foam core board; craft knife; cutting mat; beige, gold, and red acrylic paint; paintbrushes; assorted wooden stars; crackle medium; green corrugated paper; hot glue gun; assorted white buttons; one 6" and five 12" lengths of 20-gauge black craft wire; wood-tone spray; clear acrylic spray sealer; and a canvas angel without hanger.

Note: Allow paint, crackle medium, wood-tone spray, and sealer to dry after each application.

1. For frame, cut a 9" x 10¹/₂" piece from foam core board with an 8" x 9¹/₂" opening.
2. Paint stars gold and frame beige. Follow manufacturer's instructions to apply crackle medium to frame. Paint frame red.
3. Cut two ¹/₂" x 8" strips and two ¹/₂" x 9¹/₂" strips from corrugated paper. Center and glue short strips to top and bottom of frame and long strips to sides of frame. Glue stars and buttons to frame.
4. Wrap one 12" length of wire around a pencil; remove pencil. Repeat for remaining 12" lengths. Insert one end of each curled wire into top of frame. Glue one star to each remaining end. Lightly spray frame with wood-tone spray. Spray frame with sealer.
5. With 1" of wire extending above angel, center and glue 6" length of wire to back of angel. Center and insert wire extending above angel into top of frame.

CANVAS CHARACTERS (Shown on page 60)

For each character, you will need tracing paper; two 10" squares of cotton canvas fabric; one 10" square of batting; sewing thread; gesso; paintbrushes; transfer paper; pink, red, and black acrylic paint; black permanent fine-point marker; ³/₈" dia. white buttons; hot glue gun; wood-tone spray; clear acrylic spray sealer; 2"w wooden heart; fabric for heart; spray adhesive; and 10" of floral wire.
For snowman, you will **also** need orange acrylic paint.
For angel, you will **also** need white and green acrylic paint, corrugated cardboard, and household sponge.

Note: Allow gesso, paint, sealer, and wood-tone spray to dry after each application.

1. Trace patterns for desired character onto tracing paper; cut out. Draw around arm and leg or boot patterns twice and beard or body patterns once on one piece of canvas.

2. With drawn side on top, place batting between canvas pieces. Sew directly on drawn lines. Cutting close to stitching, cut out shapes. Paint one side of each piece with gesso. Use transfer paper to transfer detail lines to gesso side of pieces.
3. Paint pieces. Use marker to draw over detail lines. Sew one button to each boot or leg and arm.
4. Glue beard, arms, boots or legs to body. Apply wood-tone spray to character. Spray character with sealer.
5. For angel, trace wings pattern onto tracing paper, cut out. Draw around wings pattern on cardboard, cut out. Follow **Sponge Painting**, page 157, to lightly paint corrugated side of wings white. Glue wings to angel.
6. Draw around heart on wrong side of fabric; cut out just inside drawn line. Apply spray adhesive to wrong side of fabric heart; smooth onto wooden heart.
7. Glue arms to heart. For hanger, bend wire in half; glue ends to back of character.

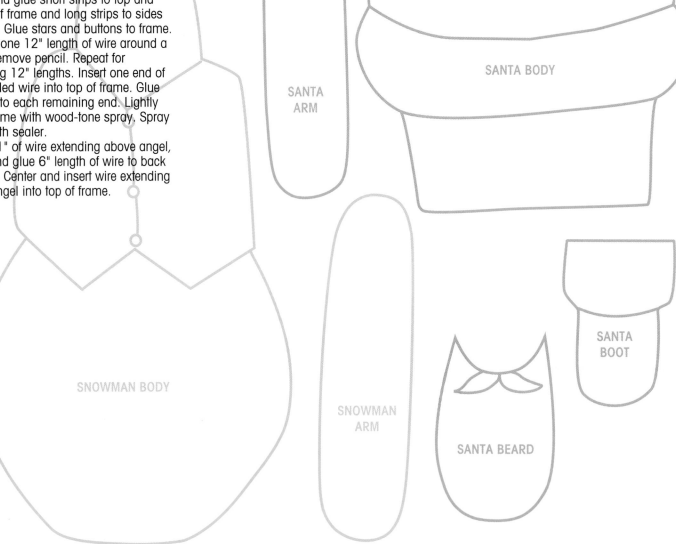

SANTA ARM

SANTA BODY

SANTA BOOT

SNOWMAN BODY

SNOWMAN ARM

SANTA BEARD

HOMEY GIFT BAGS (Shown on page 61)

BOW-TIED BAG
You will need a brown paper shopping bag, paper-backed fusible web, red-and-green print fabric, decorative-edge craft scissors, hole punch, green raffia, hot glue gun, and a 1" dia. button.

1. Measure width and height of front of bag; subtract $1/2$" from each measurement. Cut a piece of web the determined measurement.
2. Fuse web to wrong side of fabric; do not remove paper backing. Cut out fabric along edges of web. Center and fuse fabric to front of bag.
3. Use craft scissors to trim top edge of bag. Place gift in bag. Fold top of bag $2^3/4$" to front. Punch two holes 1" apart through folded part of bag. Thread several lengths of raffia through holes; tie into a bow on front of bag. Glue button to bow.

PUFFED HEART BAG
You will need paper-backed fusible web, green print fabric, kraft paper, decorative-edge craft scissors, 8" x 10" brown paper gift bag with handles, and a Puffed Heart Ornament (page 64).

1. Cut an 8" x 10" piece each of web, fabric, and kraft paper. Fuse web to wrong side of fabric; fuse fabric to kraft paper. Use craft scissors to trim short edges of rectangle.
2. Matching short edges, fold rectangle in half. Cut a slit along center of fold to fit over handles of bag. Place gift in bag. Place rectangle and ornament over handles.

STAR BAG
You will need a drawing compass, paper-backed fusible web, red print fabric, kraft paper, decorative-edge craft scissors, 8" x 10" gift bag with handles, hot glue gun, and a Star Ornament (page 67) without hanger.

1. Using compass, draw an 8" dia. circle on paper side of web; cut out. Fuse web to wrong side of fabric. Cut out fabric circle along edges of web. Fuse fabric to kraft paper. Use craft scissors to cut out circle.
2. Fold circle in half. Cut a slit along center of fold to fit over handles of bag. Place gift in bag. Place circle over handle. Glue ornament to circle and bag.

LARGE GIFT BAG
You will need large brown paper grocery bag, paper-backed fusible web, red and green print fabrics to cover bag, hot glue gun, jute twine, craft wire, wire cutters, six $3/8$" and four 1" buttons, tracing paper, kraft paper, black permanent fine-point marker, and a Cardboard and Fabric Heart Ornament (page 70).

1. Carefully pull bag apart at seams.
2. Measure height of bag; subtract 5". Measure width of bag. Cut a piece of fusible web and one piece of red fabric the determined measurements. Fuse web to wrong side of fabric. Aligning bottom of bag with one long edge of fabric, fuse fabric to bag.
3. Measure width of bag. Cut one piece of fusible web and one piece of green fabric 10" by the determined measurement. Fuse web to wrong side of fabric. Do not remove paper backing. Matching long edges, press fabric in half; unfold. Remove paper backing. Refold fabric over top of bag. Fuse fabric to inside and outside of bag.
4. Trimming to fit, glue twine to bag between red and green fabrics. Reassemble bag.
5. For handles, cut one $3/4$" x 32" piece each of green fabric and fusible web. Fuse web to wrong side of fabric. Cut fabric into four equal lengths. Cut two 8" lengths of wire. Center each wire between wrong sides of two fabric strips. Fuse fabric strips together. Glue handles to outside of bag. Glue 1" buttons to ends of handles.
6. Trace heart B pattern, page 71, onto tracing paper; cut out. Using heart B pattern and red fabric, follow **Making Appliqués**, page 156, to make six heart B appliqués. Fuse appliqués to kraft paper. Cut out hearts $1/4$" outside edges of fabric. Use marker to draw "stitches" around hearts.
7. Glue heart appliqués to front of bag. Glue $3/8$" buttons to hearts. Glue ornament to front of bag.

HAPPY HEART CHAIRS
(Shown on page 62)

MINI CHAIR
You will need a hot glue gun, one Cardboard and Fabric Heart Ornament without hanger (page 70), 5"w flat wooden heart, and a child's chair (we used a red-stained chair with a woven seat).

Note: For decorative use only.

1. Glue ornament to heart.
2. Glue heart to back of chair.

LARGE CHAIR
You will need tracing paper, craft knife, cutting mat, foam core board, ultra-thin craft steel, paper crimping tool, assorted colors of acrylic paint (we used white, yellow, red, and green), paintbrushes, hot glue gun, two 10" lengths of 20-gauge craft wire, large marker (to shape wire), two thumbtacks, ladder-back chair with a removable woven seat, fine-grit sandpaper, tack cloth, spray primer, black permanent medium-point marker, and clear acrylic spray sealer.

Note: Allow primer, paint, and sealer to dry between applications.

1. Trace heart J, heart K, page 71, star A, and star B patterns, page 70, onto tracing paper; cut out. Using patterns and craft knife, cut one heart K and one star B from foam core. Using patterns, cut one heart J and one star A from steel.
2. Use crimping tool to corrugate steel shapes. Paint foam heart and star desired colors. Glue steel shapes to foam shapes.
3. Wrap a length of wire around large marker; remove marker. Repeat with remaining wire. Insert one end of each wire into a foam shape. Wrap remaining end of each wire around a thumbtack. Insert thumbtacks into top of chair uprights.
4. Remove seat. Lightly sand chair. Wipe chair with tack cloth. Spray chair with primer. Paint desired base coats on chair.
5. Use a pencil to draw designs on chair (we drew squares, circles, hearts, and wavy lines). Paint designs. Use medium-point marker to write "Live each day with a happy ♥" on top rung of chair back. Apply two to three coats of sealer to chair. Replace seat.

WING

ANGEL ARM

ANGEL BODY

ANGEL LEG

SANTA PICKET (Shown on page 63)

You will need a handsaw; 6-ft. wooden fence picket; $^{7}/_{8}$" dia. wooden ball for nose; white, flesh, pink, red, brown, and black acrylic paint; paintbrushes; $1^{1}/_{8}$" square piece of household sponge; black permanent medium-point marker; 14" x 25" piece of red striped fabric for hat; hot glue gun; red sewing thread; $1^{3}/_{8}$" dia. jingle bell; natural raffia; two green print fabrics for patches; paper-backed fusible web; tub and tile caulk; soft cloth; 12" long greenery branch; and a Puffed Heart Ornament (page 64).

Note: Allow paint to dry after each application.

1. Use handsaw to cut 15" from top of picket. Paint picket and nose red.
2. Refer to **Fig. 1** to paint sections on picket.

Fig. 1

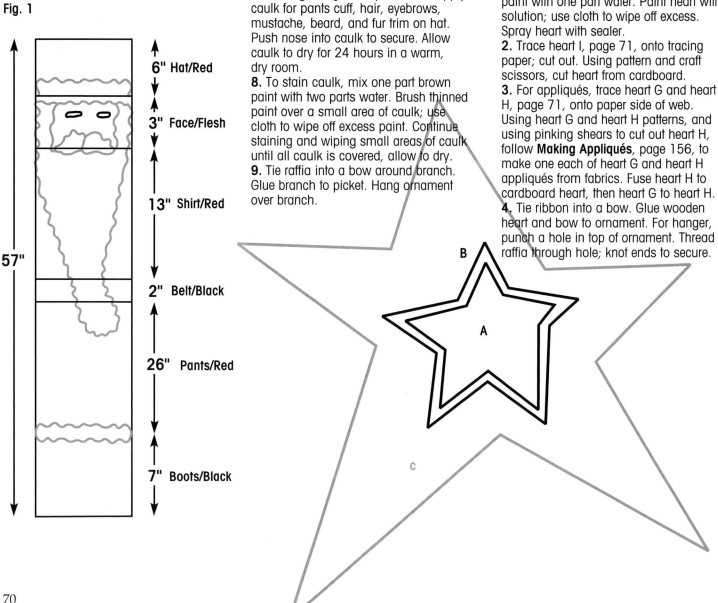

6" Hat/Red

3" Face/Flesh

13" Shirt/Red

2" Belt/Black

26" Pants/Red

7" Boots/Black

57"

B

A

C

3. Follow **Sponge Painting**, page 157, to sponge white squares in a checkerboard pattern on shirt and pants. Use white paint to highlight boots. Paint cheeks pink and eyes black; use marker to add details.
4. Aligning short end of fabric with top of face and overlapping long edges at back, glue fabric for hat to picket. Glue long edges of hat together to secure.
5. Leaving 6" thread ends, work **Running Stitch**, page 159, around top of hat. Pull thread ends to gather top of hat; knot ends to secure. Sew bell to top of hat. Tie raffia into a bow around bell. Glue side of hat to side of picket.
6. For patches, use green fabrics and follow **Making Appliqués**, page 156, to make four 2" to $2^{1}/_{2}$" square appliqués. Fuse two appliqués to front of hat. Fuse remaining appliqués to front of Santa.
7. Referring to **Fig. 1** for placement, apply caulk for pants cuff, hair, eyebrows, mustache, beard, and fur trim on hat. Push nose into caulk to secure. Allow caulk to dry for 24 hours in a warm, dry room.
8. To stain caulk, mix one part brown paint with two parts water. Brush thinned paint over a small area of caulk; use cloth to wipe off excess paint. Continue staining and wiping small areas of caulk until all caulk is covered, allow to dry.
9. Tie raffia into a bow around branch. Glue branch to picket. Hang ornament over branch.

CARDBOARD AND FABRIC HEART ORNAMENTS
(Shown on page 60)

For each ornament, you will need 1"w wooden heart, gold and brown acrylic paint, paintbrush, crackle medium, soft cloth, clear acrylic spray sealer, tracing paper, decorative-edge craft scissors, corrugated cardboard, two 5" squares each of red and green print fabrics and paper-backed fusible web, pinking shears, 10" of $^{1}/_{8}$"w green silk ribbon, hot glue gun, hole punch, and natural raffia.

Note: Allow paint and crackle medium to dry between applications.

1. Paint wooden heart gold. Follow manufacturer's instructions to apply crackle medium to wooden heart. For antiquing solution, mix one part brown paint with one part water. Paint heart with solution; use cloth to wipe off excess. Spray heart with sealer.
2. Trace heart I, page 71, onto tracing paper; cut out. Using pattern and craft scissors, cut heart from cardboard.
3. For appliqués, trace heart G and heart H, page 71, onto paper side of web. Using heart G and heart H patterns, and using pinking shears to cut out heart H, follow **Making Appliqués**, page 156, to make one each of heart G and heart H appliqués from fabrics. Fuse heart H to cardboard heart, then heart G to heart H.
4. Tie ribbon into a bow. Glue wooden heart and bow to ornament. For hanger, punch a hole in top of ornament. Thread raffia through hole; knot ends to secure.

GOOD TIDINGS

Herald the coming of the Yuletide with tastefully rustic trims from our Good Tidings collection. Skirted with an old metal ceiling panel, the artful tree combines adornments made of tea-dyed fabric and whitewashed wood to create an Early American look. You'll delight in heavenly homespun angels with tea-towel gowns and wings of decorative architectural fretwork. Spanish moss bird nests and tiny birdhouses rest on the boughs with weathered-looking ornaments crafted using unfinished wooden finials and cutouts. You'll find step-by-step instructions for these inventive projects and more beginning on page 78.

Bring good tidings to your home with a hand-embroidered **Rustic Framed Piece** *(page 81)*, stitched on linen and displayed in a whitewashed frame for bold contrast. A **Bird Nest** *(page 78)* made of Spanish moss and filled with wooden eggs adds a gentle look, and candles perched upon weathered **Candlesticks** *(page 83)* give the room a warm glow.

Our **Good Tidings Tree** *(page 78)* is a study in pioneer elegance. Whitewashed fretwork and tea-dyed table linens give these **Lacy Linen Angels** *(page 82)* the appearance of genuine antiques. Coordinating pieces include whitewashed **Wooden Ornaments** *(page 78)*, created from unfinished ornaments and wooden cutouts, and small **Birdhouses** *(page 80)*. Our Spanish moss **Bird Nests** *(page 78)* are nestled in every nook and cranny among the branches.

For a striking accent, decorate our **Good Tidings Tabletop Tree** *(page 78)* with **Angel Ornaments** *(page 79)* and star-shaped wooden ornaments. Reinforcing the old-fashioned look, a picket fence surrounds the carefully tended live tree.

Easy-to-assemble **"Noel" Pickets** *(page 78)* provide a rustic but elegant centerpiece for the mantel. One of our large birdhouses, a bird nest, an embellished candlestick, greenery, and stars complete the display. Two **Pod Garlands** *(page 80)* feature sweet gum pods, wooden star cutouts, and bay leaves.

Present your offerings in simple-to-stitch **Antiqued Gift Bags** *(page 79)* fashioned from tea-dyed linen embellished with embroidery and buttons.

Draw attention to the mantel with handmade treasures, including our **Good Tidings Wreath** *(page 78)* that's made using an angel and star ornaments from the tree. An assortment of **Candlesticks** *(page 83)*, accented with bits of evergreen, sweet gum pods, and an angel ornament, is a unique way to add cozy appeal to the room. To enhance the country feel, a medium **Birdhouse** *(page 80)* and **Bird Nest** *(page 78)* are tucked in among the heirloom adornments.

GOOD TIDINGS TREE
(Shown on page 73)

On the first Christmas, heralding angels brought the good news of God's gift to mankind. Celebrate those good tidings this year with this festive combination of country simplicity and old-fashioned elegance.

Bird Nests fashioned from Spanish moss cradle little wooden eggs, and Wooden Ornaments and Small Birdhouses (page 80) adorn the branches.

Lacy Linen Angels (page 82) robed in vintage-look raiment rest their wooden wings among the boughs. Their tea-towel dresses are lightly tea-dyed to give the illusion of age.

An antique metal ceiling panel is the perfect tree surround. The panel is cut into two long strips and painted using the **Weathered Whitewash Technique** (page 157). A hammer and nail are used to punch a hole in each corner of each strip. After the panels are bent into right angles, the short ends are wired together.

GOOD TIDINGS TABLETOP TREE
(Shown on page 75)

You will need a handsaw, four 12" x 28^1/$_2$" sections of wooden flower bed fencing, fine-grit sandpaper, tack cloth, antique white and dark brown acrylic paint, paintbrushes, paste floor wax, twelve 2"w wooden stars, hammer, nail, medium-gauge craft wire, wire cutters, wood glue, three-foot potted live evergreen, burlap to cover pot, jute twine, Wooden Ornaments (we used stars), and Angel Ornaments.

1. Use handsaw to cut 3" from each end of each fence section. Cut long pickets even with short pickets.
2. Follow **Weathered Whitewash Technique**, page 157, to paint fencing and wooden stars.
3. Use hammer and nail to punch a hole ^{1}/$_2$" from ends of railings on each fence section. Arrange sections into a square; wire together through holes. Glue wooden stars to top of every other picket; allow to dry.
4. Place tree in center of burlap. Gather burlap around pot. Knot twine around gathers to secure. Place tree in fence. Hang ornaments on tree.

BIRD NESTS
(Shown on page 74)

For each nest, you will need fine-grit sandpaper, three 1^1/$_2$"h wooden eggs, twigs, tack cloth, antique white and dark brown acrylic paint, paintbrushes, paste floor wax, drawing compass, poster board, spray adhesive, Spanish moss, and a hot glue gun.

1. Follow **Weathered Whitewash Technique**, page 157, to paint eggs and twigs.
2. For base of nest, use compass to draw a 3" dia. circle on poster board; cut out. Apply spray adhesive to one side of circle. Apply a thin layer of moss over adhesive side of circle.
3. Shape moss into a 6" dia. nest; hot glue to uncovered side of circle. Hot glue eggs and twigs to nest.

"NOEL" PICKETS
(Shown on page 76)

You will need 15^1/$_2$"h wired picket fencing, pliers, fine-grit sandpaper, tack cloth, antique white and dark brown acrylic paint, paintbrushes, paste floor wax, handsaw, hammer, and ^{1}/$_2$" long finishing nails.

1. Remove thirteen pickets from wire. Follow **Weathered Whitewash Technique**, page 157, to paint each picket.
2. Measuring from point, use handsaw to cut one 5", one 13", two 8", and four 11" lengths from pickets.
3. Refer to diagram to assemble each letter; nail to secure. Trim overlapping ends as desired.

WOODEN ORNAMENTS
(Shown on page 74)

You will need fine-grit sandpaper, tack cloth, antique white and dark brown acrylic paint, paintbrushes, and paste floor wax.
For each finial ornament, you will also need a wooden finial ornament (we used 5^1/$_8$"h and 6^1/$_4$"h ornaments), craft drill, eye screw, and 8" of ^{1}/$_8$"w white satin ribbon.
For each star ornament, you will also need a ^{1}/$_2$"-thick, 3^1/$_2$"w wooden star; 5" of floral wire; and a hot glue gun.

1. For each ornament, follow **Weathered Whitewash Technique**, page 157, to paint desired wooden shape.
2. For finial ornament hanger, drill hole in top of shape. Screw eye screw into hole. Thread ribbon through screw and knot ends together.
3. For star ornament hanger, bend wire in half; glue ends to back of star.

GOOD TIDINGS WREATH
(Shown on page 77)

You will need fine-grit sandpaper, tack cloth, antique white and dark brown acrylic paint, paintbrushes, paste floor wax, six 1^1/$_2$"w and three 3^1/$_2$"w wooden stars, hot glue gun, bay leaves, dried Queen Anne's lace, 24" dia. twig wreath, floral wire, wire cutters, artificial greenery with berries, sweet gum pods, and a large Lacy Linen Angel (page 82).

1. Follow **Weathered Whitewash Technique**, page 157, to paint stars.
2. Arrange and glue bay leaves, Queen Anne's Lace, and stars on wreath. Wire greenery, pods, and angel to wreath.

DIAGRAM

ANTIQUED GIFT BAGS (Shown on page 77)

Note: Using six strands of floss for French Knots and three strands of floss for all other stitches, follow **Embroidery Stitches**, page 158, for all embroidery stitches.

SMALL GIFT BAG

You will need a tea bag; 6" cutwork linen square; two 6" plain linen squares with 1"w finished edges; tracing paper; green and brown embroidery floss; one $7/8$" dia., one $3/8$" dia., and two $1/2$" dia. buttons; and 14" of $1/8$"w ecru ribbon.

1. Follow **Tea Dyeing**, page 156, to dye linen squares.
2. Trace flower pattern onto tracing paper. Pin pattern onto center right side of one plain square. Work Backstitches and Straight Stitches to embroider design; carefully remove paper. Using green floss, center and sew $7/8$" dia. button $23/8$" from bottom edge.
3. Place embroidered square right side up on second plain square. Using a 1" seam allowance and leaving top edge open, sew squares together.
4. For flap, fold cutwork square in half diagonally. Place top edges of bag inside fold; pin back of flap in place. Using green floss, sew a $1/2$" dia. button through back corner of flap and back of bag; remove pins.
5. Fold ribbon in half; pin fold to front corner of flap. Sew remaining $1/2$" dia. button to flap and fold of ribbon. Sew $3/8$" dia. button to flap above $1/2$" dia. button. Tie ribbon into a bow around 1" dia. button.

MEDIUM GIFT BAG

You will need a tea bag, two $81/2$" lace-edged linen squares, tracing paper, brown embroidery floss, assorted buttons, and two 24" lengths of $1/8$"w ecru ribbon.

1. Follow **Tea Dyeing**, page 156, to dye linen squares.
2. Trace the word "joy" from Rustic Framed Piece pattern, page 80, onto tracing paper. Pin pattern onto lower left corner of one linen square. Work a French Knot and Running Stitches to embroider design; carefully remove paper. Sew three buttons to embroidered square.
3. Matching wrong sides and leaving top edge open, sew squares together along inside edge of lace.
4. Working through both thicknesses of lace, use six strands of brown floss to tie buttons to bottom and side edges of bag.
5. Leaving equal lengths of ribbon at each side of bag, weave one ribbon length through lace along each top edge.
6. At each side, knot ribbons together close to bag and again 2" from ends. Thread ribbon ends through button and knot ends together to secure.

LARGE GIFT BAG

You will need a tea bag, a 14" x 18" lace-edged tea towel, tracing paper, green and brown embroidery floss, assorted buttons, 1 yd. of $1/4$"w ecru ribbon.

1. Follow **Tea Dyeing**, page 156, to dye towel.
2. Matching wrong sides, fold lace edge down 6". Stitch across towel $5/8$" from fold to form casing at top.
3. Matching right sides and short edges, fold towel in half. Using a $5/8$" seam allowance, sew across bottom edge of towel. Turn right side out.
4. Trace "good tidings" from Rustic Framed Piece pattern, page 81, onto tracing paper. Pin design 3" from bottom edge on front side of bag. Work Backstitches, French Knots, and Running Stitches to embroider design; carefully remove paper. Sew three buttons below design.
5. Using green floss and adding a button at every third stitch, work Running Stitches along side edge of casing.
6. Thread ribbon through casing; knot a button onto each end of ribbon. Use green floss to sew button below casing.

ANGEL ORNAMENT
(Shown on page 75)

You will need fine-grit sandpaper, $33/4$" x $77/8$" decorative wooden house trim, $11/2$"w wooden star, tack cloth, antique white and dark brown acrylic paint, paintbrushes, paste floor wax, a tea bag, 5" x 6" piece of muslin, 4" of 1"w ecru crocheted lace with $3/4$"w bias tape edge, tracing paper, transfer paper, 12" of medium-gauge craft wire, hot glue gun, jumbo craft stick, polyester fiberfill, brown embroidery floss, two 4mm black beads, utility scissors, assorted buttons, and poster board.

1. Follow **Weathered Whitewash Technique**, page 157, to paint trim and star. Follow **Tea Dyeing**, page 156, to dye muslin and lace.
2. Trace angel head A or B pattern, page 82, onto tracing paper. Matching short edges, fold muslin in half. Using pattern, cut head from muslin. Leaving bottom edges open, use a $1/4$" seam allowance to sew head pieces together. Clip curves and turn right side out. Use transfer paper to transfer face pattern onto head.
3. Form a $1/2$" loop at one end of craft wire. Glue loop to one side at end of craft stick. Working wire out through top of head, insert craft stick into head. Stuff head with fiberfill around craft stick. Glue opening closed around craft stick.
4. Using three strands of floss to stitch face, insert needle in fabric $1/2$" from starting point; bring needle up at starting point. Pull thread to "pop" knot through fabric; stitch face. Knot floss close to fabric and "pop" knot into batting; clip floss close to fabric. Sew beads to face for eyes.
5. Use utility scissors to trim craft stick even with bottom edge of head. Glue lace around neck to form collar. Glue one button to center of collar.
6. For "hair" buttons, knot a length of floss at front of each button. Glue regular and "hair" buttons to head.
7. Glue angel to trim piece.
8. Draw around star on poster board; cut out. Glue wooden star and poster board star together over wire. Bend wire to form hanger.

FLOWER PATTERN

BIRDHOUSES
(Shown on pages 74, 76, and 77)

Note: Allow glue to dry after each application. Clamp pieces as necessary while drying.

SMALL BIRDHOUSE
You will need utility scissors, 1/4"w decorative-edge wooden dollhouse trim, wood glue, wooden birdhouse (we used a 2 1/2"d x 3 1/4"w x 5 1/4"h birdhouse), fine-grit sandpaper, tack cloth, antique white and dark brown acrylic paint, paintbrushes, paste floor wax, and 10" of floral wire.

1. Use scissors to cut pieces of trim to fit along edges of birdhouse; glue in place.
2. Follow **Weathered Whitewash Technique**, page 157, to paint house.
3. For hanger, bend wire in half; glue ends to back of house.

MEDIUM BIRDHOUSE
You will need utility scissors, 3/8"w decorative-edge wooden dollhouse trim, papier-mâché birdhouse (we used a 7"d x 6"w x 6"h birdhouse), wood glue, three 3 1/2" long wooden craft picks, one 10mm and two 8mm wooden beads, fine-grit sandpaper, tack cloth, antique white and dark brown acrylic paint, paintbrushes, and paste floor wax.

1. Use scissors to cut pieces of trim to fit along edges of birdhouse; glue in place.
2. Measuring from pointed ends, cut one 1 1/2" and two 1" lengths from craft picks. Glue an 8mm bead on each 1" length and 10mm bead on 1 1/2" length. Glue 1 1/2" length to point of roof and one 1" length to each front corner of base of birdhouse.
3. Follow **Weathered Whitewash Technique**, page 157, to paint house.

LARGE BIRDHOUSE
You will need utility scissors, 3/8"w decorative-edge and 3/8"w flat bead wooden dollhouse trim, wood glue, wooden birdhouse (we used a 7"d x 7"w x 9 1/2"h birdhouse), 3 1/2"h turned wooden cone, fine-grit sandpaper, tack cloth, antique white and dark brown acrylic paint, paintbrushes, and paste floor wax.

1. Use scissors to cut pieces of trim to fit along edges of birdhouse; glue in place.
2. Glue cone to top of roof.
3. Follow **Weathered Whitewash Technique**, page 157, to paint house.

POD GARLANDS (Shown on page 76)

For each garland, you will need 2 yds. of string, a long sharp needle, and sweet gum pods.
For starry garland, you will also need fine-grit sandpaper; 1/2"-thick, 3 1/2"w wooden star shapes; craft drill; tack cloth; antique white and dark brown acrylic paint; paintbrushes; paste floor wax; and bay leaves.

SWEET GUM POD GARLAND
1. Thread and tie a sweet gum pod onto one end of string. Continue threading pods onto string to 6" from end of string.
2. Knot string end around nearest pod to secure.

STARRY GARLAND
1. Follow **Weathered Whitewash Technique**, page 157, to paint stars. Drill a hole through one point on each star.
2. Thread and tie a sweet gum pod onto one end of string. Thread leaves onto string for 14".
3. Thread a pod, a star, a pod, and 14" of leaves onto string. Continue threading in this order, ending with a pod. Knot string end around nearest pod to secure.

RUSTIC FRAMED PIECE (Shown on page 72)

You will need a tea bag; 3" of ¹/₂"w ecru crocheted lace; vinegar; ecru, green, brown and dark brown embroidery floss; 10" x 13" piece of water-soluble stabilizer; 16" x 19" piece of 32 ct Belfast linen; tracing paper; muslin; transfer paper; batting; paper-backed fusible web; assorted white print fabric scraps; two 4mm black beads; assorted buttons; hot glue gun, fine-grit sandpaper, 1³/₄"w wooden frame with 9¹/₂" x 12¹/₂" opening for inner frame; wooden frame with 12¹/₂" x 15¹/₂" opening for outer frame; tack cloth; antique white and dark brown acrylic paint; paintbrushes; and paste floor wax.

Note: Use three strands of floss and follow **Embroidery Stitches**, page 158, for all embroidery stitches unless otherwise indicated.

1. Follow **Tea Dyeing,** page 156, to dye lace. For each floss color, mix 1 tablespoon vinegar in 8 ounces clear water. Soak floss in mixture to release excess dye; allow to air dry.
2. Aligning arrows and dashed lines, trace pattern onto stabilizer. Center stabilizer on linen; baste in place.
3. Trace angel head A pattern, page 82, onto tracing paper; trim 1¹/₄" from bottom of pattern. Using pattern, cut head from muslin ¹/₄" outside pattern edge; press edges ¹/₄" to wrong side. Use transfer paper to transfer face to head.
4. Cut a piece of batting slightly smaller than head. With batting on wrong side of head, place head on stabilizer. Hand stitch head to stabilizer and linen.
5. Work Backstitches, Cross Stitches, French Knots, Running Stitches, and Straight Stitches to embroider design. Use brown floss for face, wings, and halo; green floss for branches; and ecru floss for Cross Stitches. Use two strands of dark brown floss for verse and six strands of dark brown floss for French Knots.
6. Follow manufacturer's instructions to dissolve stabilizer.
7. Fuse web to wrong side of fabric scraps. Trace stars from pattern onto tracing paper; cut out. Use patterns to cut stars from fused scraps. Fuse stars in place. Sew beads to head for eyes. Turning ends under to fit, tack lace at neck.
8. For "hair" buttons, knot a length of floss at front of each button. Glue regular and "hair" buttons to head. Glue a button to halo. Glue three buttons to stitched piece.
9. Follow **Weathered Whitewash Technique**, page 157, to paint frames. Glue outer frame over inner frame. Mount stitched piece in frame.

RUSTIC FRAMED PIECE

good tidings
which
all people.
Luke 2:10

LACY LINEN ANGELS (Shown on page 74)

Note: Use a 1/4" seam allowance for all sewing unless otherwise indicated.

SMALL ANGEL

You will need fine-grit sandpaper, two 5 1/2"w wooden hearts, two 3 3/4" wooden craft spoons for arms, tack cloth, antique white and dark brown acrylic paint, paintbrushes, paste floor wax, a tea bag, muslin, 14" x 22" lace-trimmed tea towel, 3" of 1 1/2"w crocheted lace, tracing paper, transfer paper, 10" of craft wire, hot glue gun, jumbo craft stick, polyester fiberfill, ecru and brown embroidery floss, two 4mm black beads, assorted buttons, utility scissors, straight pins, 2" x 5" block of 1 1/4"-thick plastic foam, and 20" of 3/8"w ecru satin ribbon.

1. Follow **Weathered Whitewash Technique**, page 157, to paint hearts and spoons. Follow **Tea Dyeing**, page 156, to dye muslin, towel, and lace.

2. Follow Steps 2 - 4 and 6 of Angel Ornaments, page 79, to make head. Use utility scissors to trim stick to a point. Insert stick into one short end of foam block.

3. For dress, matching right sides and short edges, fold towel in half. Mark fold on each side with a pin; unfold. Cut two 3" pieces of 1/2"w lace. Matching center of lace to pin, topstitch one lace piece to each side of towel; refold towel. Beginning at ends of lace, stitch side seams. Cut a 1" slit along center of fold for neck opening. Turn dress right side out and place on angel.

4. Tack buttons to bodice of dress. Glue 1 1/2"w lace around neck for collar.

5. Knot ribbon around waist to form sleeves; knot ribbon ends. Glue one arm into each sleeve and button to knot of ribbon.

6. Bend wire to form halo. Glue button to halo.

7. Glue hearts to back of dress for wings. Using ecru floss, work **Running Stitches**, page 159, along bottom edge of skirt. Pull floss ends to loosely gather; knot ends to secure.

MEDIUM ANGEL

You will need fine-grit sandpaper, 2 3/4" x 12 1/2" decorative wooden trim, two regular craft sticks for arms, tack cloth, antique white and dark brown acrylic paint, paintbrushes, paste floor wax, a tea bag, muslin, three 14" x 22" lace-edged tea towels, 8" of 3"w flat lace, three 2 1/2" lengths of 1/4"w crocheted lace, tracing paper, transfer paper, 10" of craft wire, hot glue gun, jumbo craft stick, polyester fiberfill, brown embroidery floss, two 4mm black beads, assorted buttons, utility scissors, and a 2 3/4" x 3 7/8" plastic foam egg.

BODICE

1. Follow **Weathered Whitewash Technique**, page 157, to paint wooden trim and regular craft sticks. Follow **Tea Dyeing**, page 156, to dye muslin, towels, lace trims, and lace.

2. Follow Steps 2 - 4 and 6 of Angel Ornaments, page 79, to make head. Use utility scissors to trim stick to a point. Insert stick into large end of egg.

3. Follow **Making Patterns**, page 156, to make bodice pattern. Matching short edges, fold one towel in half. Aligning top edge of pattern with fold of towel; pin pattern in place. Cut out bodice. Matching ends of 3"w lace to bottom edges of bodice, center and stitch lace to bodice. Trim lace from neck opening.

4. Measuring from lace edge, cut each remaining towel to 14" long. Sew two rows of gathering threads along cut edge of each towel. Matching right sides and gathering to fit, sew one towel to each bottom edge of bodice. Matching right sides, sew each side seam from sleeve opening to bottom of skirt. Turn dress right side out and place on angel.

5. Lightly stuff sleeves with fiberfill. Glue one arm into each sleeve. Knot floss around each arm to form wrist. Trimming to fit and covering floss, glue a piece of crocheted lace around each sleeve; glue a length of lace around neck for collar.

6. Bend wire to form halo. Glue button to halo.

7. Glue trim to back of dress for wings.

LARGE ANGEL

You will need wood glue; three 8" wooden brackets; 3/8"-thick, 3" x 3 7/8" wooden block; four jumbo craft sticks; utility scissors; fine-grit sandpaper; tack cloth; antique white and dark brown acrylic paint; paintbrushes; paste floor wax; a tea bag; muslin; 15" x 34" linen runner; two 6" Battenberg lace doilies; tracing paper; transfer paper; 10" of craft wire; polyester fiberfill; hot glue gun; brown embroidery floss; two 4mm black beads; assorted 1/2" dia. buttons; 3" x 4" block of 1"-thick plastic foam; batting; removable fabric marking pen; craft knife; cutting mat; one 1 1/2" dia. button; and two 30" lengths of 1/4"w ecru satin ribbon.

1. Referring to Wing Diagram, use wood glue to glue brackets and block together to form wings. Cut one craft stick into four pieces; glue to back of wings at seams for support. Allow to dry.

2. For arms, use utility scissors to trim one end of two craft sticks to a blunt point. Follow **Weathered Whitewash Technique**, page 157, to paint wings and arms. Follow **Tea Dyeing**, page 156, to dye muslin, runner, and lace doilies.

3. Using angel head C pattern, follow Steps 2 - 4 and 6 of Angel Ornaments, page 79, to make head. Use utility scissors to trim stick to a point. Insert stick into one short end of foam block. Glue batting around foam.

4. Matching right sides and short edges, fold runner in half. Following Dress Diagram, draw lines for sewing dress on folded runner. Stitch along drawn lines. Cut out dress 1/4" outside stitching lines. Cut a 1 1/2" wide curve at center of fold for neck opening. Clip seam at underarm. Turn dress right side out and place on angel.

5. Fold sleeves to front of dress; spot glue together to secure. Glue one arm into each sleeve. Drape one doily over each shoulder to form collar; glue to secure.

6. Tack 1 1/2" dia. button at neck and several 1/2" dia. buttons to dress.

7. Tie ribbons together into a small bow; knot ends. Tack bow to dress below button at neck.

8. Bend wire to form halo. Glue button to halo.

9. Glue wings to back of angel.

ANGEL HEAD A

ANGEL HEAD B

ANGEL HEAD C

WING DIAGRAM

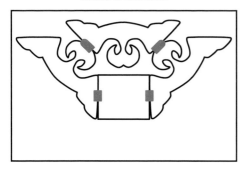

DRESS DIAGRAM

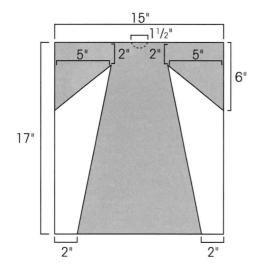

CANDLESTICKS (Shown on page 77)

Note: Use wood glue for all gluing unless otherwise indicated. Allow glue to dry after each application.

SMALL CANDLESTICK

You will need a craft drill, $3^3/4$" decorative resin square, 7" French Gothic fence post finial, $1^1/2$" long wood screw, screwdriver, fine-grit sandpaper, tack cloth, antique white and dark brown acrylic paint, paintbrushes, paste floor wax, wood-tone spray, and a 3" dia. pillar candle.

1. For candlestick base, drill a hole through center of decorative square and 1" deep in top center of finial. Use wood screw to attach square to top of finial.
2. Follow **Weathered Whitewash Technique**, page 157, to paint candlestick.
3. Spray candle lightly with wood tone spray; allow to dry. Screw candle onto candlestick.

MEDIUM CANDLESTICK

You will need an 18" long decorative wooden table leg with square top, craft saw, craft drill, $1^1/2$" long wood screw, screwdriver, $4^1/2$" square flat wooden post cap, utility scissors, $1/4$"w and $1/2$"w decorative-edge wooden dollhouse trim, wood glue, $3^1/4$" dia. wooden Shaker box lid, pliers, $1/4$" x $2^1/2$" dowel screw, fine-grit sandpaper, tack cloth, antique white and dark brown acrylic paint, paintbrushes, paste floor wax, 3" dia. pillar candle, wood-tone spray, hot glue gun, three sweet gum pods, artificial cedar sprig with berries, and 8" of floral wire.

1. Mark leg 12" from square end. Using saw and cutting in groove closest to mark, cut tapered end from leg. Drill a hole 1" deep in center of square end of leg. For candlestick base, use wood screw to attach top of post cap to square end of leg.
2. Measure width of square end of leg. Use utility scissors to cut four pieces of $1/2$"w trim $1/8$" longer than the determined measurement. Cut four pieces of $1/4$"w trim $1/4$" longer than determined measurement. Glue $1/2$"w trim pieces, then $1/4$"w trim pieces around square end of leg.

3. Center and glue top of box lid on top of leg. Drill a hole 1" deep in center of top of candlestick. Leaving one half of screw exposed, use pliers to insert dowel screw in hole.
4. Follow **Weathered Whitewash Technique**, page 157, to paint candlestick.
5. Spray candle lightly with wood tone spray; allow to dry. Screw candle onto candlestick.
6. Use hot glue to glue sweet gum pods to cedar. Wire cedar to candlestick.

LARGE CANDLESTICK

You will need an 18" long decorative wooden table leg with square top, craft saw, craft drill, $1^1/2$" long wood screw, screwdriver, $4^1/2$" square flat wooden post cap, miter box, $1/2$"w crown molding for dollhouses, wood glue, $3^3/4$" decorative resin square, $2^1/4$" dia. wooden Shaker box lid, $1/4$" x $2^1/2$" dowel screw, pliers, fine-grit sandpaper, tack cloth, antique white and dark brown acrylic paint, paintbrushes, paste floor wax, 2" dia. pillar candle, wood-tone spray, ecru thread, and one Angel Ornament (page 79).

1. Mark leg 18" from square end. Use saw to cut tapered end from leg at mark. Drill a hole 1" deep in center of square end of leg. For candlestick base, use wood screw to attach top of post cap to square end of leg.
2. Measure width of square end of leg; add $1/8$". Using craft saw and 45° angle of miter box, cut four pieces of molding with inside edge the determined measurement. Glue molding pieces around square end of leg.
3. Center and glue decorative square, then top of box lid on top of leg. Drill a hole 1" deep in center of top of candlestick. Leaving one half of screw exposed, use pliers to insert dowel screw in hole.
4. Follow **Weathered Whitewash Technique**, page 157, to paint candlestick.
5. Spray candle lightly with wood tone spray; allow to dry. Screw candle onto candlestick. Use thread to hang ornament on candlestick.

"BEARY" SWEET NATIVITY

Here's a whimsical re-creation custom-made for teddy bear collectors — the coming of the Christ Child is depicted with cute, cuddly teddy bears dressed up as the Holy Family! Soft felt robes and traditional headcloths adorn Mary and Joseph, and the sweet face of Baby Jesus peeks out from cozy swaddling clothes tied up with raffia. You won't be able to resist making this "beary" sweet trio!

HOLY FAMILY

MARY

You will need tracing paper, 18" x 21½" piece of blue felt, pinking shears, 12"h jointed teddy bear, hot glue gun, 1 yd. of 1"w blue wired ribbon, blue fabric dye, white tea towel with Battenberg lace edging, straight pins, and 18" of ½"w blue picot-edged satin ribbon.

1. For robe pattern, cut a 9" x 10¾" piece from tracing paper. Refer to **Fig. 1** to draw pattern on tracing paper; cut out.

Fig. 1

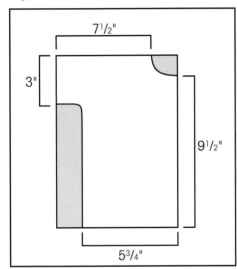

2. Matching short edges, fold felt in half from top to bottom. Fold again from right to left. Refer to **Fig. 2** for pattern placement. Cut out sides and underarms. Use pinking shears to cut out neck and trim sleeves and bottom edges of robe.

Fig. 2

3. Use a ¼" seam allowance to sew each side seam from ends of sleeves to bottom edges of robe. Turn robe right side out. Use pinking shears to cut robe down center front from neck to bottom edge (**Fig. 3**).

Fig. 3

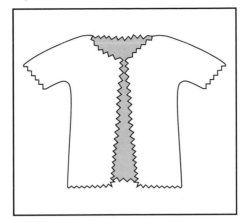

4. Fold sleeves 1½" to right side for cuffs. Press one opening edge of robe ½" to right side. Place robe on bear. Overlapping left side over right side, glue robe front closed.

5. Wrap wired ribbon around bear and knot at back. Bring ribbon ends around bear and knot in front.

6. For headcloth, follow manufacturer's instructions to dye towel; press. Measuring from lace edge, cut towel to 12" long. Press cut edge ¼" to wrong side; press ¼" to wrong side again. Stitch in place.

7. Drape headcloth over bear's head with lace edge on top. Pull ears through openings in lace; pin to secure. Gather lace edge of headcloth at neck; pin to secure. Knotting at back of head, tie satin ribbon around ears.

JOSEPH

You will need tracing paper, pinking shears, 18" x 21½" piece of green felt, 12"h jointed teddy bear, hot glue gun, 1 yd. of 2"w green moiré ribbon, one 14" square each of white fabric and green print fabric, craft knife, cutting mat, 18" of ¼" dia. green twisted cord, and round box or can for stand (we used a 3⅞" dia. x 4⅝"h papier-mâché box).

1. Using green felt, follow Steps 1 - 3 of Mary to make robe.

2. Fold sleeves 1½" to right side for cuffs. Press one opening edge of robe ¾" to right side. Place robe on bear. Overlapping left side over right side, glue robe front closed.

3. Using moiré ribbon, follow Step 5 of Mary to tie ribbon around bear.

4. For headcloth, matching right sides and leaving an opening for turning, use a ¼" seam allowance to sew fabric squares together. Turn right side out. Hand sew opening closed; press.

5. Place headcloth on bear and mark position of ears. Remove headcloth. Use craft knife to cut a slit for each ear. Inserting bear's ears through slits, replace headcloth. Knotting cord ends together at back and gluing to secure, wrap cord around ears.

6. Place Joseph's feet in box or can.

BABY JESUS

You will need pinking shears, 16" square of cotton batting, 6"h teddy bear, and natural raffia.

1. Use pinking shears to trim edges of batting. Place bear right side up on batting with head 4" from one corner.

2. Wrap remaining three corners tightly around bear. Crisscrossing raffia several times before knotting, wrap raffia around bear and batting; knot to secure. Tuck top corner of batting under bear's head.

CRIMSON AND ICE

Enrich your home's interior with the warmth of deep crimson and the icy crispness of white in this collection. At the center of the radiant display is a poinsettia-covered tree sprinkled with snowflakes, icicles, and other winter treasures. Sharing the spotlight are exquisite topiaries and luxurious embossed velvet accessories. You'll also marvel at garlands of frosty flowers and branches and packages tied up with big shimmery bows. You can create this snowy Christmas wonderland using the project instructions beginning on page 90.

Slip something special into our **Embossed Velvet Stocking** *(page 93)*! It's elegantly embellished with a snow-white cuff and trimmed with a gold tassel.

An **Embossed Velvet Pillow** *(page 90)* featuring gold fringe and dimensional paint highlights will warm up any nook or cranny.

Our **Crimson and Ice Tree** *(page 90)* is dressed up in glittering **Frosted Glass Ornaments** *(page 90)*, elegant **Snow-Edged Poinsettias** *(page 91)*, and shiny **Red Berry Ornaments** *(page 90)*. Decorative **Bow-Tied Tassels** *(page 91)* and eye-catching **Shimmering Snowflakes** *(page 91)* are among the adornments. Purchased garlands of jewels and icicles, along with icicle ornaments and clear glass orbs filled with shredded white Mylar™, add frosty flair to this exquisite evergreen.

Make a bold holiday statement with a centerpiece created using a striking **Beaded Topiary** *(page 92)*, a round **Poinsettia Topiary** *(page 92)*, and a hand-painted **Hurricane Candle Holder** *(page 92)* that features a frosty snowflake design. Surround these unique accents with festive **Floral Arrangements** *(page 92)* and **Frosted Glass Ornaments** *(page 90)*, made using white paint and glitter. White globe candles and wintertime garlands complete this feast for the eyes.

CRIMSON AND ICE TREE
(Shown on page 87)

Crisp, powdery snowfalls and the warming glow of the hearth – these are the images brought to mind by this crimson-and-ice tree. Bead and icicle garlands wind around its 7½-foot height. More icicles along with golden glass teardrops sparkle among the branches.

Bright Frosted Glass Ornaments gleam in three different designs and sizes. Shiny Red Berry Ornaments and glistening Snow-Edged Poinsettias nestle beside Shimmering Snowflakes and Bow-Tied Tassels. Clear glass ornaments filled with shredded white Mylar™ reflect the glow of a jacquard fabric "snowdrift" beneath the tree.

RED BERRY ORNAMENTS
(Shown on page 88)

For each ornament, you will need red spray paint, 2" dia. plastic foam ball, 10" of ⅝"w gold mesh wired ribbon, floral pin, artificial frosted juniper sprigs, wired artificial red berry picks, wire cutters, hot glue gun, and red and white bead garland.

1. Spray paint foam ball; allow to dry.
2. For hanger, fold ribbon in half to make a loop. Use floral pin to pin loop and three juniper sprigs to top of ball.
3. Leaving ½" stems, use wire cutters to cut berries from picks. Apply glue to each stem and insert in ball to cover ball.
4. Cut beads from garland. Glue beads and additional juniper sprigs to top of ornament.

FROSTED GLASS ORNAMENTS
(Shown on page 88)

SMALL ORNAMENT
You will need white dimensional paint, 2¼" dia. red glass ornament, and white crystal glitter.

Paint a "snowcap" over top of ornament. Generously sprinkle glitter over wet paint; allow to dry. Gently shake ornament to remove excess glitter.

MEDIUM ORNAMENT
You will need water-based crystal glaze, 2½" dia. red glass ornament, fine iridescent glitter, artificial variegated holly pick, and a hot glue gun.

1. Drip glaze over top of ornament. Sprinkle glitter over wet glaze; allow to dry. Gently shake ornament to remove excess glitter.
2. Remove five leaves from pick. Glue leaves around ornament cap.

LARGE ORNAMENT
You will need a craft stick, white dimensional paint, 4" dia. red glass ornament, an artificial dusty miller stem, hot glue gun, and 14" of 2½"w sheer white wired ribbon.

1. Use craft stick to apply paint to each leaf and top half of ornament; allow to dry.
2. Use paint to make dots on and below painted area of ornament.
3. Remove six leaves from stem. Glue leaves around ornament cap. Tie ribbon into a bow through hanger on ornament.

EMBOSSED VELVET PILLOW
(Shown on page 88)

You will need tracing paper, carbon paper, linoleum printing block, colored pencil, carving tools with medium and large U-shaped cutting blades, old toothbrush, chalk, 20" x 25" piece and a scrap piece of red 100% rayon velvet, polyester fiberfill, 25" of 6"w gold bullion fringe, fabric glue, and gold glitter dimensional paint.

1. Follow **Embossing Velvet**, page 156, to prepare velvet.
2. Matching right sides and short edges, fold velvet in half. Using a ½" seam allowance and leaving an opening for turning, sew raw edges together. Turn pillow right side out. Stuff pillow with fiberfill. Sew opening closed.
3. Cut fringe into two 12½" lengths. Turning cut ends of fringe under ¼" to wrong side, glue a length of fringe along each end of pillow; allow to dry.
4. Dot paint in center of each embossed design; allow to dry.

EMBOSSING PATTERN

SHIMMERING SNOWFLAKES
(Shown on page 88)

For each ornament, you will need tracing paper, tape, clear shrinking plastic, white dimensional paint, ultra-fine iridescent glitter, sharp needle, and 6" of clear nylon thread.

1. Trace desired snowflake pattern onto tracing paper. Tape pattern to work surface. Tape plastic over pattern. Paint over lines of pattern on plastic. Sprinkle wet paint with glitter; allow to dry. Gently shake plastic to remove excess glitter.
2. Cut snowflake from plastic. Use needle to pierce snowflake and pull thread through hole; knot ends together.

SNOW-EDGED POINSETTIAS
(Shown on page 88)

For each poinsettia, you will need wire cutters, 9" dia. red artificial poinsettia stem, floral tape, dimensional paint applicator, Aleene's™ True Snow, and coarsely cut iridescent glitter.

1. Use wire cutters to trim stem to 5" long. Wrap stem with floral tape.
2. Fill applicator with True Snow. Apply a line of "snow" along edges of red leaves and on tips of green leaves. Sprinkle glitter over wet snow; allow to dry. Gently shake poinsettia to remove excess glitter.

BOW-TIED TASSELS
(Shown on page 88)

For each tassel, you will need 24" of 1/8" dia. pre-strung clear iridescent beads, 6" white tassel, hot glue gun, 1"w red and gold braid, and 16" of 1 1/4"w red wired ribbon with gold edges.

1. Cut bead strand into six 4" lengths. Working around tassel below knot, glue one end of each string to tassel. Covering ends of beads, glue braid around top of tassel.
2. Tie ribbon into a bow around hanger of tassel; notch ends.

SNOWFLAKES

BEADED TOPIARY

(Shown on page 89)

You will need red spray paint; 16"h plastic foam cone; 5" dia. terra-cotta flowerpot; wood-tone spray; floral foam; hot glue gun; utility knife; 18" of $1/2$" dia. dowel rod; 18" of $5/8$"w white satin ribbon; $2^3/4$ yds. each of white and red bead garland, $1/4$" dia. velvet cord with $1/2$" lip, and $1/8$" dia. satin twist cord; two plastic foam snowflake ornaments; two white foam berry picks; fiberfill; snow texture paint; paintbrush; artificial snow; artificial holly pick; $1^1/4$"w red velvet wired ribbon with gold edges; spray adhesive; and 25" of $3/8$"w red velveteen cord.

Note: Allow paint and wood-tone spray to dry after each application.

1. Spray paint cone and flowerpot red. Lightly spray flowerpot with wood-tone spray. Fill pot with floral foam; glue to secure. Use utility knife to carefully shape each end of dowel to a point. Apply glue to one end of dowel; insert in center of pot. Apply glue to opposite end of dowel. Leaving 4" of dowel exposed for trunk, insert dowel in bottom of cone. Gluing ends to secure, wrap trunk with satin ribbon.

2. Beginning at top of cone and gluing in place, wind velvet cord, satin cord, and bead garland around cone. Glue one snowflake and one berry pick to top of cone.

3. Glue fiberfill over foam in pot. Paint fiberfill with texture paint. Sprinkle artificial snow over wet paint. Insert holly and remaining berry pick in flowerpot. Tie wired ribbon into a bow. Glue bow and remaining snowflake to flowerpot.

4. Lightly apply spray adhesive to topiary; sprinkle with artificial snow.

5. Knot ends of velveteen cord. Form three loops at center of cord; knot one streamer around center of loops. Glue bow to top of cone.

POINSETTIA TOPIARY

(Shown on page 89)

You will need red spray paint, $3^1/2$" dia. x 5"h terra-cotta flowerpot, floral foam, hot glue gun, spray adhesive, 6" dia. plastic foam ball, sheet moss, several 15" lengths of frosted twigs, fiberfill, snow texture paint, paintbrush, white plastic foam berry picks, artificial snow, flocked artificial holly picks, seven 9" dia. red artificial poinsettias, and 25" of $3/8$"w red velveteen cord.

Note: Allow paint to dry after each application unless otherwise indicated.

1. Spray paint flowerpot red. Fill pot with floral foam; glue to secure. Apply spray adhesive to foam ball; cover with moss.

2. For trunk, apply glue to one end of each twig and insert in center of pot. Leaving 6" exposed, insert remaining ends into ball.

3. Glue fiberfill over foam in pot. Paint fiberfill with texture paint. Sprinkle artificial snow over wet paint. Insert holly and white berry picks in pot.

4. Remove leaves from poinsettias. Beginning near bottom, arranging leaves from largest to smallest and overlapping as necessary, glue leaves to ball. Insert holly picks in top and bottom of ball. Insert remaining berry picks in top of ball.

5. Lightly apply spray adhesive to topiary and sprinkle with artificial snow.

6. Knot ends of velveteen cord. Form three loops at center of cord; knot one streamer around center of loops. Glue bow to top of ball.

FLORAL ARRANGEMENTS

(Shown on page 89)

For each arrangement, you will need floral pins, a 6"w triangle of 1" thick white plastic foam, artificial juniper sprigs, one Snow-Edged Poinsettia without green leaves (page 91), and white twigs.

1. Using floral pins to secure, cover foam with juniper.

2. Insert poinsettia at center of foam.

3. Using floral pins, arrange and secure juniper sprigs and white twigs around edges of poinsettia.

HURRICANE CANDLE HOLDER

(Shown on page 89)

You will need tracing paper, tape, 6" dia. x 7"h hurricane globe with gold stand, white dimensional paint, ultra-fine iridescent glitter, and a red pillar candle.

1. Trace large snowflake pattern onto tracing paper. Tape pattern inside globe.

2. Paint over lines of pattern on outside of globe. Sprinkle wet paint with glitter; allow to dry. Gently shake globe to remove excess glitter. Remove pattern. Place candle in globe.

STOCKING CUFF

EMBOSSED VELVET STOCKING (Shown on page 86)

You will need tracing paper, carbon paper, linoleum printing block, colored pencil, carving tools with medium and large U-shaped cutting blades, old toothbrush, chalk, 18" x 24" piece and a scrap of red 100% rayon velvet, 18" x 24" piece of white satin for lining, 10" x 28" piece of white satin for cuffs, two 18" lengths of 1/8" dia. gold cord with lip, 12" of 1/8" dia. twisted gold cord, 5" gold bead tassel, and gold glitter dimensional paint.

Note: Use a 1/4" seam allowance for all sewing, unless otherwise indicated.

1. Using embossing pattern, page 90, follow **Embossing Velvet**, page 156, to prepare velvet.

2. Aligning arrows and dotted lines, trace stocking top and stocking bottom patterns onto tracing paper. For seam allowance, draw a second line 1/4" outside first line around sides and bottom of stocking. Cut out pattern along outer line.

3. Matching right sides and short edges, fold velvet in half. Using pattern, cut stocking pieces from velvet. Repeat using satin for lining.

4. Leaving top edges open, sew stocking pieces together. Clip curves and turn stocking right side out. Repeat to sew lining pieces together; do not turn.

5. Follow **Making Patterns**, page 156, to trace cuff pattern onto tracing paper; cut out. Matching short edges, fold satin for cuffs in half. Matching long edges, fold in half again. Using pattern, cut four cuffs from satin. Matching lip with raw edge,

baste one 18" length of cord along curved edge on right side of one cuff piece. Repeat using remaining cord length and a second cuff piece.

6. Matching right sides and using a zipper foot, sew one cuff with cord to one plain cuff along curved edge; turn right side out. Repeat using remaining cuff pieces.

7. Place lining inside stocking. Place one cuff inside lining with center of cuff at toe seam; pin in place. Place second cuff inside lining with center at heel seam; pin in place. With raw edges even, sew stocking and cuffs together. Pull cuff out from stocking. Topstitch seam in place. Fold cuff down over stocking.

8. For hanger, knot ends of twisted cord together. Sew knot of hanger inside stocking at heel seam. Tack tassel to cuff on front of stocking.

9. Dot paint in centers of each embossed design; allow to dry.

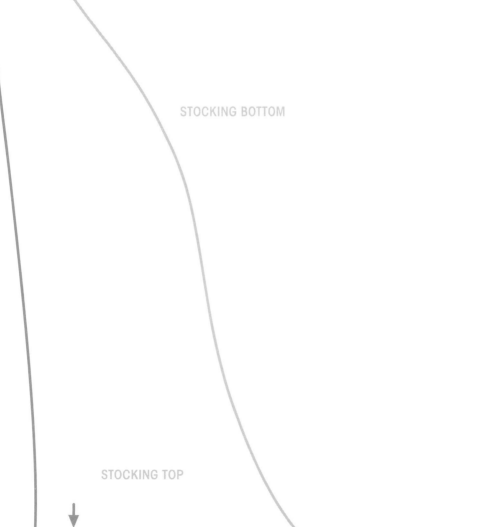

STOCKING BOTTOM

STOCKING TOP

THE SHARING OF CHRISTMAS

*One of the greatest joys
of Christmastime is sharing
goodwill with others. We've
lovingly gathered a selection of
ideas for creative gift-giving, from
accents for the home to merry
wearables and festive edibles. Express
your thoughtfulness with folksy
appliquéd coasters, a cross-stitched
shirt, or a spirited cheese log.
Remember Dad with a handsome
desk set, and Mother can preserve
memories in a tapestry-covered
album. Whoever you're thinking
of, there's something crafty
and unique in the pages of
this fabulous collection!*

*F*ill a basket with folksy appliquéd **Heart Coasters** (page 106) to please a country-loving friend! Pull your favorite fabrics out of the scrap box to make the fused-on hearts; finish with basic embroidery stitches.

*S*hare down-home holiday cheer with this **"Warm Wishes" Card Holder** (page 106). The wall hanging is easy to make with no machine-sewing involved — just fuse together and add embroidered embellishments.

Displayed on the front door, our hand-painted **Skating Santa Sled** (page 110)
offers a whimsical greeting to all. What a great gift for a special family!

*R*ock-a-bye Santa, it's Christmas Eve! Dress baby in holiday style with a sweet cross-stitched **Santa Patch** (page 109). Sew the quick-to-stitch "patch" on a little one's romper, or add festive fun to a diaper bag or blanket.

*T*o create this clever **Snowman Dress** (page 114), just add an appliquéd felt skirt to a ready-made T-shirt. A young miss will love wearing the frosty party dress!

*S*anta Claus is coming to town! Use your imagination — and our colorful cross-stitched **Santa Patches** (page 109) — to add a Christmasy touch to a variety of ready-to-wear items such as the overalls and shirt shown here. Your creativity will be a hit with all ages.

*P*erfect for a parent or grandparent, this decorative **Memory Plate** (page 113) showcases decoupaged photographs of loved ones.

*S*ewn from richly colored fabric and trimmed in gold, a set of **Ornament Place Mats** (page 108) will bring an elegant look to a friend's dining table.

Wrapped with plaid ribbon, a ready-made pillow becomes a festive "package." The jewel-like blossom on our **Poinsettia Pillow** (page 113) is easy to craft from lengths of wired ribbon.

More ribbon flowers transform a store-bought chenille throw into a stunning **Poinsettia Afghan** (page 113).

Whether the mood is subtle chic or vibrant cheer, this reversible **Crocheted Vest** (page 112) makes a fashionable statement! The vest is worked entirely in simple single crochet stitches, so it's easy enough for even a beginning crocheter to make.

*E*veryone will think you found this luxurious **Covered Album** (page 111) at an exclusive gift shop! It's actually affordable to create by covering a plain photo album with tapestry fabric.

*H*andsomely attired in stock-market style, our **Masculine Desk Set** (page 108) will please a business-minded gentleman. The decoupaged photo frame, pencil holder, and storage box are trimmed with buttons and cording in neutral tones.

Send "Season's Greetings" with a bottle of **Creamy Mocha Liqueur** (page 115). *The **Velvet Gift Bag** (page 114) is embossed with a holiday message and tied with greenery and gilded acorn ornaments.*

104

*D*elicious with turkey or ham, sweet and savory **Raspberry-Mustard Spread** and **Red Onion Jam** (page 115) make great gifts for neighbors. Festive wrapping paper brings a holiday glow to the **Bow-Tied Gift Bags and Jar Toppers** (page 115).

*A*pricot brandy adds spirit to this elegant **Apricot Cheese Log** (page 115). To treat a special couple, pack the almond-coated log and a bag of crackers in a gilded **Gift Basket** (page 115).

"WARM WISHES" CARD HOLDER (Shown on page 96)

You will need 21¹/₂" of ¹/₂" dia. wooden dowel, green acrylic paint, paintbrush, two 2¹/₄"w wooden stars, assorted gold and red print fabrics, fabric glue, paper-backed fusible web, 18" x 40" piece of ecru felt, red and green embroidery floss, three 5" squares of assorted tan print fabrics, pinking shears, tracing paper, transfer paper, 3" x 11" piece of tan felt, 12" x 12" piece of red felt, 5" x 13" piece of green felt, four red ¹/₂"w buttons, floral wire, wire cutters, and a hot glue gun.

Note: Refer to **Embroidery Stitches**, page 158, and use six strands of green floss for all Running Stitches and three strands of red floss for all Blanket Stitches. Stitch through all layers for all embroidery stitches. Use fabric glue for all gluing unless otherwise indicated.

1. Paint dowel green. Trace around wooden stars on wrong side of gold fabric; cut out. Glue fabric stars to wooden stars.
2. Cut an 18" x 20" piece of web. Matching one 18" edge of ecru felt with one 18" edge of web, fuse web to felt. Remove paper backing and fold unfused side of felt over web; fuse felt layers together. Work Running Stitches along folded edge of felt.
3. For pocket, fold stitched edge 5¹/₂" to one side (front). Work Running Stitches along all outer edges of card holder and 6" from each side edge of pocket.
4. Fuse web to wrong side of each tan fabric square. Use pinking shears to trim edges of squares. Fuse squares to pockets.

5. Follow **Making Appliqués**, page 156, to make three heart A appliqués from red felt, three heart B and two heart C appliqués from red fabric, and five star appliqués from gold fabric. Fuse heart B appliqués to heart A appliqués. Work Blanket Stitches around each heart B appliqué. Fuse heart A appliqués to pockets.
6. For sign, trace the words "Warm Wishes" onto tracing paper; transfer words to tan felt. Work Running Stitches over transferred lines. Glue sign to red felt. Leaving a ¹/₄" red border, use pinking shears to cut out sign.
7. Matching arrows and dotted lines, trace outer border A and outer border B onto tracing paper. Using pattern, cut outer border from green felt. Center and glue sign to outer border. Center and glue outer border to card holder 1¹/₂" below top edge. Fuse heart C appliqués and stars to card holder.
8. For hanging loops, cut a 2" x 26" strip of red fabric and a 1" x 26" strip of web. Center and fuse web strip to wrong side of fabric strip. Remove paper backing and fold long edges of fabric ¹/₂" to wrong side; fuse in place. Use pinking shears to trim ends of strip and cut strip into four 6" lengths; fold each length in half. With ends at front and back of card holder and spacing loops evenly across top, use red floss to sew buttons and loops to card holder.
9. Insert dowel through loops. Hot glue center of a 5" length of wire to back of each wooden star. Wire one star to each end of dowel; hot glue to secure.

HEART COASTERS
(Shown on page 96)

For each coaster, you will need paper-backed fusible web; one 5¹/₂" square each of red felt, green felt, and beige print fabric; 4¹/₂" square of gold, red, or green print fabric; 2" square of yellow print fabric; red embroidery floss; and pinking shears.

1. Fuse web to wrong side of each fabric square and red felt.
2. Follow **Making Appliqués**, page 156, to make one heart A from red felt, one heart B from gold, red, or green fabric, and one star from yellow fabric.
3. Fuse heart B to heart A. Fuse star to heart B. Using six strands of floss and stitching through both layers, work **Blanket Stitches**, page 158, around edges of heart B. Fuse heart A to beige square.
4. Leaving a ¹/₄" beige border, use pinking shears to trim edges of beige square. Center and fuse beige square to green felt. Using six strands of floss, work **Running Stitches**, page 159, along edges of beige square.

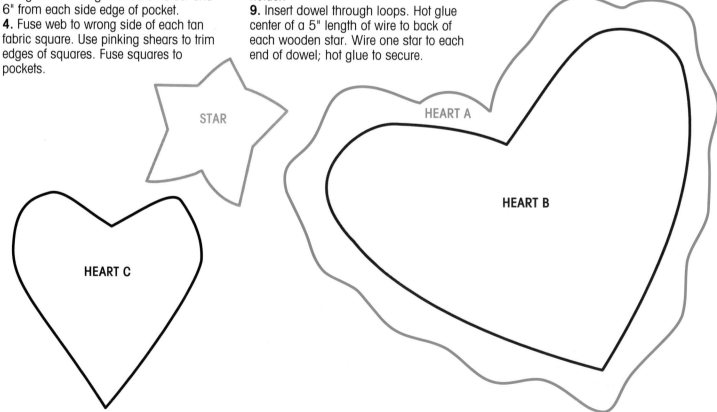

STAR

HEART A

HEART B

HEART C

Warm

Wishes

ORNAMENT PLACE MATS
(Shown on page 100)

For one place mat, you will need tracing paper, two 16" x 20" pieces of fabric for place mat front and backing, one 16" x 20" piece of batting, 20" of 1¹/₂"w decorative ribbon with gold edges, 1¹/₂ yds. of gold twist cord with lip, and 16" of 1¹/₂"w gold mesh wired ribbon.

1. Aligning arrows and dotted lines, trace place mat A and place mat B patterns onto tracing paper; cut out. Using pattern, follow **Making Patterns**, page 156, to make full-size place mat pattern. Cutting ¹/₂" outside edges of pattern, cut shape from fabrics and batting.
2. Arrange and sew decorative ribbon on right side of place mat front.
3. Beginning at top and matching raw edges, baste lip of cord on right side of place mat front.
4. Place backing fabric right side up on batting. With right sides together, position place mat front on backing. Leaving an opening for turning and using a zipper foot, sew layers together as close as possible to cording. Clip curves and trim seam allowance to ¹/₄". Turn right side out and sew opening closed.
5. Press place mat. Tie gold ribbon into a bow. Tack bow at top of place mat.

PLACE MAT B

MASCULINE DESK SET (Shown on page 103)

Note: Allow paint, wood-tone spray, and sealer to dry after each application. We used stock market report newsprint to cover projects.

FRAME
You will need a frame with stand, newsprint, spray adhesive, wood-tone spray, clear acrylic spray sealer, hot glue gun, ³/₈" dia. brown satin cord, and assorted buttons.

1. Measure length and width of one long side of frame; add 2" to each measurement. Cut two strips of newsprint the determined measurements. Apply spray adhesive to wrong side of strips. Center one strip on one long side of frame. From inside opening of frame, make a clip at each corner. Smooth strip onto sides and around to back of frame. Repeat for opposite side.
2. Measure length and width of one short side of frame; add 2" to width measurement. Cut two strips of newsprint the determined measurements. Apply spray adhesive to wrong side of strips. Center one strip on one short side of frame. Fold short ends of strip diagonally to wrong side to fit frame opening. Smooth strip around sides and onto back of frame. Repeat for opposite side.
3. Apply wood-tone spray, then sealer to frame.
4. Tie a knot in one end of cord. Beginning with knot at center top of frame and trimming to fit, glue cord around sides of frame. Glue buttons to frame.

PENCIL CUP
You will need brown spray paint, clean empty can, newsprint, spray adhesive, wood-tone spray, clear acrylic spray sealer, ³/₈" dia. brown satin cord, hot glue gun, and assorted buttons.

1. Spray paint inside and outside of can. Measure around can; add ¹/₂". Measure height of can between rims. Cut a piece of newsprint the determined measurements. Apply spray adhesive to wrong side of paper. Overlapping ends, smooth paper around can.
2. Apply wood-tone spray, then sealer to can.
3. Tie a knot in one end of cord. Beginning with knot at top front of can and trimming to fit, glue cord around can. Glue buttons to can.

BOX
You will need newsprint, an empty cardboard box with lid, spray adhesive, wood-tone spray, clear acrylic spray sealer, ³/₈" dia. brown satin cord, hot glue gun, and assorted buttons.

1. Cut a piece of newsprint large enough to cover box lid. Apply spray adhesive to wrong side of newsprint. Center lid on wrong side of newsprint. Pleating as necessary, smooth newsprint over sides to inside of lid. Repeat to cover bottom of box.
2. Apply wood-tone spray, then sealer to box and lid.
3. Tie a knot in one end of cord. Beginning with knot at center front of lid and trimming to fit, glue cord around top of lid. Glue buttons to box.

PLACE MAT A

SANTA PATCHES

(Shown on pages 98 and 99)

For each patch, you will need a 6" square each of white Aida (14 ct) and desired color felt, embroidery floss (see color key), paper-backed fusible web, pinking shears, and purchased garment.

Note: Refer to **Cross Stitch**, page 158, before beginning project. Use 3 strands of floss for Cross Stitch and 1 strand for Backstitch unless otherwise indicated.

1. Center and work desired Santa design on Aida.

2. Fuse web to wrong side of stitched piece. Trim edges of stitched piece to one thread outside Cross Stitch border. Fuse stitched piece to center of felt. Leaving a ¹/₂" felt border, use pinking shears to trim patch.

3. Pin patch to garment. Sewing inside Cross Stitch border, sew patch to garment.

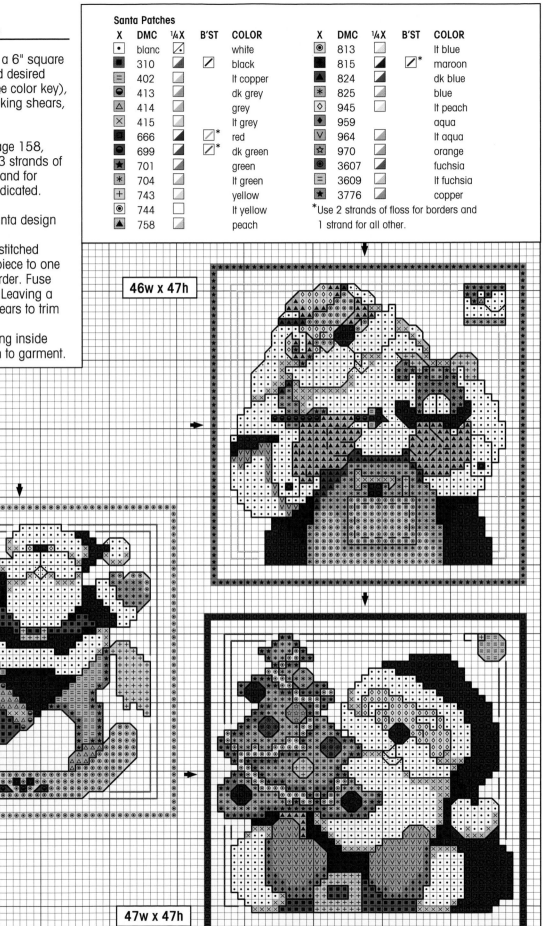

Santa Patches

X	DMC	¼X	B'ST	COLOR		X	DMC	¼X	B'ST	COLOR
•	blanc			white		⊙	813			lt blue
■	310		▞	black		■	815		▞*	maroon
⊟	402			lt copper		▲	824			dk blue
◉	413			dk grey		✱	825			blue
△	414			grey		◇	945			lt peach
✕	415			lt grey		◆	959			aqua
■	666		▞*	red		∨	964			lt aqua
◓	699		▞*	dk green		☆	970			orange
★	701			green		◉	3607			fuchsia
✳	704			lt green		⊜	3609			lt fuchsia
+	743			yellow		★	3776			copper
⊙	744			lt yellow						
▲	758			peach						

*Use 2 strands of floss for borders and 1 strand for all other.

46w x 47h

46w x 46h

47w x 47h

109

SKATING SANTA SLED (Shown on page 97)

You will need sandpaper; an unfinished wooden sled with an area 8³/₄" x 13¹/₂" or larger for painting; two 2"w wooden stars; tack cloth; clear satin varnish; soft cloth; walnut stain; white, antique white, yellow, dark yellow, flesh, red, grey blue, navy blue, brown, and black acrylic paint; paintbrushes; tracing paper; graphite transfer paper; pencil; kraft paper; tape; old toothbrush; matte acrylic spray sealer; two yds. of 2¹/₂"w wired ribbon; floral wire; wire cutters; artificial greenery; twigs; hot glue gun; and three pinecones.

Note: Refer to **Painting Techniques**, page 157, before beginning project. Allow stain, varnish, paint, and sealer to dry after each application unless otherwise indicated. To thin paint, mix one part paint to one part water. Use graphite transfer paper when transferring designs.

1. Sand sled and stars. Use tack cloth to remove dust. Apply varnish to sled and stars. Sand again and remove dust. Use

soft cloth to apply stain to stars and sled runners.
2. Excluding runners, paint sled red. Paint stars dark yellow.
3. Aligning arrows and dotted lines, trace Sled A and Sled B patterns onto tracing paper. Transfer oval outline to sled and to center of a piece of kraft paper large enough to cover sled. Paint oval on sled navy blue.

SLED A

110

4. Transfer "ice" line to sled. Follow **Painting Techniques** to float thinned white paint across, then down "ice."
5. Transfer remaining design to sled. Refer to photo and follow **Painting Techniques** to paint Santa.
6. Cut transferred oval from kraft paper; discard oval. Covering red background, position opening in kraft paper over painted design; secure with tape. Cover Santa's face with a piece of kraft paper; secure with tape. Use toothbrush to spatter thinned white paint over exposed area of oval. Remove paper. Spatter thinned yellow and brown paint over stars.
7. Paint wavy line and dot border. Spray sled and stars with sealer.
8. Follow **Making a Bow**, page 156, and use ribbon to make a bow with four 8" loops, one 16" streamer, and one 24" streamer. Notch ribbon ends. Wire greenery and twigs to sled. Wire bow to greenery. Glue stars and pinecones to greenery and bow. Glue streamers to runners.

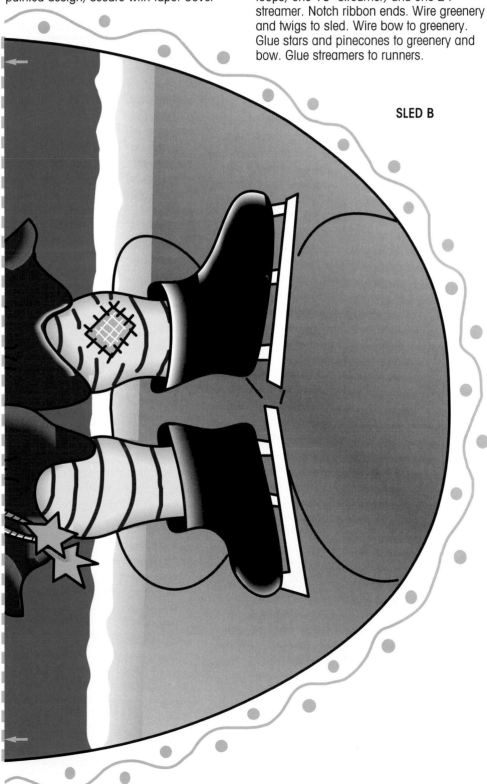

SLED B

COVERED ALBUM
(Shown on page 103)

You will need tapestry fabric to cover album, photo album with center rings, hot glue gun, 1¹/₄"w wired ribbon, ¹/₂"w gold braid, fabric glue, ⁵/₈"w wired ribbon, poster board, fabric for lining, large nail, hammer, and tassel.

Note: Use hot glue for all gluing unless otherwise indicated.

1. Cut a piece of fabric for cover 2" larger on all sides than opened album. Center opened album on wrong side of fabric piece.
2. Fold corners of fabric diagonally over corners of album; glue in place. Fold short edges of fabric over side edges of album; glue in place. Fold long edges of fabric over edges of album, trimming fabric to fit ¹/₄" under binding hardware; glue in place.
3. Cut two 3"w tapestry fabric strips ¹/₂" shorter than height of album. Press ends of each strip ¹/₄" to wrong side. On inside of album, center and glue one strip along each side of binding hardware with one long edge of each strip tucked ¹/₄" under hardware.
4. Cut one length each of 1¹/₄"w ribbon and braid 2" longer than width of open album. Glue braid along center of ribbon.
5. Use fabric glue to glue ribbon around album, gluing ends to inside front and back covers.
6. For ribbon tie closure, cut two 10" lengths of ⁵/₈"w ribbon. Center and glue one end of each ribbon length to inside front and back of album on long opening edge.
7. For liners, cut two pieces of poster board 1" smaller on all sides than front of album. Cut two pieces of fabric for lining 2" larger than poster board pieces. Center one poster board piece on wrong side of one fabric piece. Fold corners of fabric piece diagonally over corners of poster board; glue in place. Fold edges of fabric over edges of poster board; glue in place. Repeat with remaining poster board and fabric. Glue liners to insides of covers.
8. Use hammer and nail to punch a hole through front album cover at center of long opening edge. Insert tassel hanger through hole from inside to outside of album and pull up a loop. Insert tassel through loop and pull tightly.
9. Tie long ribbon ends together into a bow.

CROCHETED VEST (Shown on page 102)

Vest Size	Finished Chest
Small	40"
Medium	44"
Large	48"

Instructions are written for size Small with sizes Medium and Large in braces {}. If only one number is given, it applies to all sizes.

You will need size E crochet hook or size needed for gauge, yarn needle, and sport weight yarn in the following colors and amounts:
Color A (tan) - 6{7-8} ounces
Color B (rust) - 2¹/₂{3-3} ounces
Color C (teal) - 2{2-2¹/₂} ounces

Note: Read **Changing Colors** before beginning the vest and follow **Stripe Sequence** to work vest.

CHANGING COLORS
Change color in the last sc of the row **before** the row which is to be worked in the new color.
To work color change, insert hook in last sc of row, YO and pull up a loop, drop yarn, with new yarn, YO and draw through both loops on hook **(Fig. 1)**. Cut old yarn and work over both ends.

Fig. 1

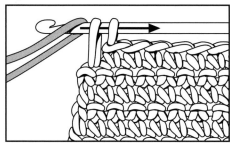

STRIPE SEQUENCE
Sizes small and medium only
Work one row of **each** color: ★ Color A **(Fig. 1)**, Color B, Color A, Color C; repeat from ★ throughout.

Size large only
Work one row of **each** color: Color A **(Fig. 1)**, Color B, Color A, ★ Color C, Color A, Color B, Color A; repeat from ★ throughout.

Gauge: 18 sc and 22 rows = 4"

BODY
Ch 181{199-217} **loosely**.
Row 1 (Right side)**:** Sc in second ch from hook and in each ch across: 180{198-216} sc.
Note: Loop a short piece of yarn around any stitch to mark last row as **right** side.
Rows 2-52: Ch 1, turn; sc in each sc across. Do **not** finish off.

RIGHT FRONT
Row 53: Ch 1, turn; sc in first 38{43-48} sc, leave remaining 142{155-168} sc unworked.
Rows 54 and 55: Ch 1, turn; sc in each sc across to last 2 sc, skip next sc, sc in last sc: 36{41-46} sc.
Row 56: Ch 1, turn; sc in each sc across.
Rows 57-59: Ch 1, turn; sc in each sc across to last 2 sc, skip next sc, sc in last sc: 33{38-43} sc.
Rows 60-63: Repeat Rows 56-59: 30{35-40} sc.
Rows 64 and 65: Ch 1, turn; sc in each sc across.
Row 66: Ch 1, turn; sc in each sc across to last 2 sc, skip next sc, sc in last sc: 29{34-39} sc.
Rows 67-69: Ch 1, turn; sc in each sc across.
Rows 70-89{97-105}: Repeat Rows 66-69, 5{7-9} times: 24{27-30} sc.
Row 90{98-106}: Ch 1, turn; sc in each sc across to last 2 sc, skip next sc, sc in last sc: 23{26-29} sc.
Rows 91{99-107} thru 104{108-111}: Ch 1, turn; sc in each sc across. Finish off leaving a long end for sewing.

BACK
Row 53: With **right** side facing and working in unworked sc on Row 52, skip first 12 sc from Right Front and join yarn with slip st in next sc; ch 1, sc in same st and in next 79{87-95} sc, leave remaining 50{55-60} sc unworked: 80{88-96} sc.
Row 54: Ch 1, turn; sc in each sc across.
Row 55: Ch 1, turn; skip first sc, sc in next sc and in each sc across to last 2 sc, skip next sc, sc in last sc: 78{86-94} sc.
Rows 56-63: Repeat Rows 54 and 55, 4 times: 70{78-86} sc.
Rows 64-104{108-111}: Ch 1, turn; sc in each sc across.
Finish off.

LEFT FRONT
Row 53: With **right** side facing and working in unworked sc on Row 52, skip first 12 sc from Back and join yarn with slip st in next sc; ch 1, sc in same st and in each sc across: 38{43-48} sc.
Rows 54 and 55: Ch 1, turn; skip first sc, sc in next sc and in each sc across: 36{41-46} sc.
Row 56: Ch 1, turn; sc in each sc across.
Rows 57-59: Ch 1, turn; skip first sc, sc in next sc and in each sc across: 33{38-43} sc.
Rows 60-63: Repeat Rows 56-59: 30{35-40} sc.
Rows 64 and 65: Ch 1, turn; sc in each sc across.
Row 66: Ch 1, turn; skip first sc, sc in next sc and in each sc across: 29{34-39} sc.
Rows 67-69: Ch 1, turn; sc in each sc across.
Rows 70-89{97-105}: Repeat Rows 66-69, 5{7-9} times: 24{27-30} sc.
Row 90{98-106}: Ch 1, turn; skip first sc, sc in next sc and in each sc across: 23{26-29} sc.
Rows 91{99-107} thru 104{108-111}: Ch 1, turn; sc in each sc across. Finish off leaving a long end for sewing. Sew shoulder seams **(Fig. 2)**.

Fig. 2

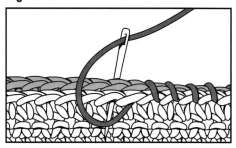

EDGING
Rnd 1: With **right** side facing, join Color A with slip st in any sc at center of Back neck edge; ch 1, sc evenly around working 3 sc in each corner; join with slip st to first sc, finish off.

ARMHOLE EDGING
Rnd 1: With **right** side facing, join Color A with slip st in any sc at underarm; ch 1, sc evenly around; join with slip st to first sc, finish off.

Repeat for second Armhole.

POINSETTIA AFGHAN (Shown on page 101)

You will need straight pins, five 44" lengths of 1¹/₂"w red wired ribbon, sewing thread to match ribbons, five 18" lengths of ¹/₂"w gold satin ribbon, seven 7" lengths of 1¹/₂"w green wired ribbon, and an afghan (we used a 48" square green chenille afghan with fringe).

1. For each poinsettia, use pins to mark one red ribbon length at 2³/₄" intervals (**Fig. 1**).

Fig. 1

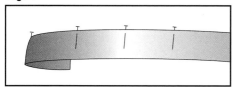

2. Fold one end of ribbon to wrong side at first pin, placing raw end under second pin. Remove second pin; pinch folded ribbon. Wrap gathers tightly with thread. (**Fig. 2**). Continue folding ribbon at pins, pinching ribbon and wrapping with thread to make eight petals (**Fig. 3**). Remove all pins.

Fig. 2

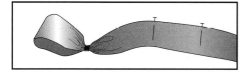

Fig. 3

3. Spread petals apart. At folded end of each petal, fold corners to back of petal. Stitch folds together.
4. For center of flower, tie ten to twelve knots in one gold ribbon length. Arrange knots in a spiral with raw ends underneath. Stitch to center of petals.
5. For each leaf, matching ends, fold one green ribbon length in half. Wrap ends with thread. At folded end of leaf, fold corners to back of petal. Stitch folds together.
6. Repeat Steps 1 - 5 to make five flowers and seven leaves. Stitch one or two leaves to back of each flower. Stitch flowers to afghan.

POINSETTIA PILLOW
(Shown on page 101)

You will need 2¹/₄"w wired ribbon to wrap around pillow, purchased pillow (we used a 12" x 17" pillow), 44" length of 1¹/₂"w red wired ribbon, sewing thread to match ribbons, 18" of ¹/₂"w gold ribbon, and a 7" length of green wired ribbon.

1. Crisscrossing center of ribbon at back, wrap 2¹/₄"w ribbon around width and length of pillow; tie ends into a bow.
2. Follow Steps 1 - 5 of Poinsettia Afghan and use remaining ribbons to make one poinsettia and one leaf. Stitch leaf to back of poinsettia. Stitch poinsettia to knot of bow.

MEMORY PLATE
(Shown on page 100)

You will need tracing paper; transfer paper; green card stock; light red, red, light green, and green permanent medium-point markers; ¹/₁₆" hole punch; decorative-edge craft scissors; color photocopies of photographs; decoupage glue; 10³/₄" dia. clear glass plate; sponge pieces; red acrylic paint; paintbrushes; adhesive size; gold leaf; and clear acrylic spray sealer.

Note: Allow glue, paint, and sealer to dry after each application. Plate is intended for decorative use only.

1. Trace center design and heart D patterns onto tracing paper; cut out. Use transfer paper to transfer design to card stock. Use markers to draw over transferred lines. Punch evenly spaced holes in a circle around design. Cutting ¹/₄" outside punched holes, use craft scissors to cut out circle. Using heart pattern and craft scissors, cut out photocopies.
2. Use foam brush to apply decoupage glue to right side of center design and photocopies; arrange on back of plate and smooth in place.
3. Use damp sponge to lightly apply red paint over back of plate (do not apply a solid coat of paint). Follow manufacturers' instructions to apply adhesive size and gold leaf over back of plate.
4. Spray back of plate with sealer.

CENTER DESIGN

HEART D

SNOWMAN DRESS (Shown on page 98)

For a girl's size 5 dress, you will need a size 6-8 black T-shirt, 42" square of white felt, tracing paper, orange and black felt, orange and black embroidery floss, $1/4$"w elastic, and 9" x 44" strip of fabric for sash.

1. Press hem of T-shirt $4^1/2$" to wrong side. Leaving a small opening along bottom edge of hem to insert elastic, sew close to top and bottom of hem to make casing.
2. Using a 6" measurement for inside cutting line and a 21" measurement for outside cutting line, follow **Cutting a Fabric Circle**, page 156, to cut skirt from white felt.
3. Match inside opening edge of skirt to pressed edge on right side of T-shirt. Easing to fit and using $1/2$" seam allowance, sew skirt to T-shirt.

4. Trace face patterns onto tracing paper; cut out. Using patterns, cut one nose from orange felt and two eyes and five mouth pieces from black felt. Use matching color floss and long stitches to sew face pieces to skirt.
5. Measure child's waist; add 1". Cut a length of elastic the determined measurement. Thread elastic through casing. Sew elastic ends together. Sew opening closed.
6. For sash, matching right sides and long edges, fold fabric strip in half. Leaving an opening for turning and using a $1/2$" seam allowance, sew raw edges of fabric strip together. Turn sash right side out. Sew opening closed and press.

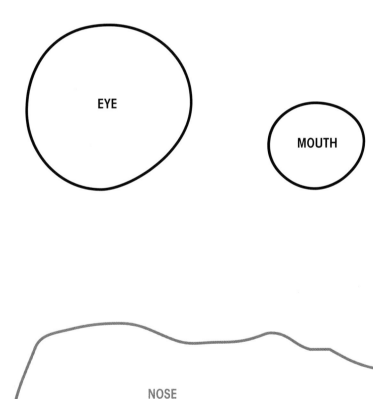

VELVET GIFT BAG
(Shown on page 104)

You will need a 19" x 21" piece of rayon velvet, "Season's Greetings" and pine bough rubber stamps, fine-point gold paint pen, gold glitter dimensional fabric paint, two acorn ornaments with hangers, 30" of $3/8$" dia. gold twist cord, and an artificial greenery sprig.

Note: Allow paint to dry after each application. Use a $1/4$" seam allowance for all sewing.

1. Follow Steps 4 and 5 of **Embossing Velvet**, page 156, and use rubber stamps in place of block to emboss "Season's Greetings" 6" from one short edge of velvet. Emboss bough design on each side of words.
2. Use paint pen to draw over designs on right side of velvet. Use dimensional paint to highlight designs.
3. Matching right sides of velvet, sew long edges together. With seam at center back, sew across one short edge for bottom of bag.
4. Refer to **Fig. 1** to sew across each corner of bag $1^1/2$" from ends. Trim ends to $1/4$" from seam. Fold top edge of bag 3" to wrong side; sew in place. Turn bag right side out.

Fig. 1

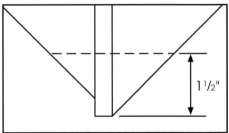

5. Place gift in bag. Thread ornaments onto cord. Tie cord into a bow around top of bag. Insert greenery under knot of bow.

CREAMY MOCHA LIQUEUR
(Shown on page 104)

  1 can (14 ounces) sweetened
      condensed milk
  1 cup whipping cream
  1 cup coffee-flavored liqueur
 1/2 cup chocolate-flavored liqueur

Pour sweetened condensed milk, whipping cream, and liqueurs in a blender. Process until blended. Pour into gift bottle. Store in refrigerator. Serve chilled.
Yield: about $3^2/_3$ cups liqueur

BOW-TIED GIFT BAGS AND JAR TOPPERS
(Shown on page 105)

You will need wrapping paper, red raffia, ecru card stock, black permanent fine-point marker, spray adhesive, lunch-size brown paper bags, decorative-edge craft scissors, hole punch, and $1^1/_4$"w gold mesh wired ribbon.

1. For each jar topper, draw around lid on wrong side of wrapping paper. Cutting 2" outside drawn line, cut out circle. Place paper over lid; knot a length of raffia around lid to secure.
2. For each jar label, cut a 1" square of card stock. Use marker to write recipe name on square. Apply spray adhesive to wrong side of label. Smooth label onto top of jar.
3. For each gift bag, measure front of bag. Cut a piece of wrapping paper the determined measurements. Apply spray adhesive to wrong side of paper. Smooth paper onto front of bag. Use craft scissors to trim top of bag.
4. Place gift in bag. Fold top of bag $1^1/_2$" to front. Punch two holes 1" apart in center of folded part of bag. Thread an 18" length of ribbon through holes; tie ends into a bow.

RASPBERRY-MUSTARD SPREAD (Shown on page 105)

  1 jar (12 ounces) seedless raspberry
      jam
  3 tablespoons Dijon-style mustard
  2 tablespoons honey

Place jam in a microwave-safe medium bowl. Microwave on high power (100%) 1 minute or until jam melts. Stir in mustard and honey. Spoon jam into jars with lids. Store in refrigerator.
Yield: about $1^1/_4$ cups spread

RED ONION JAM
(Shown on page 105)

  3 cups finely chopped red onions
      (about 1 pound onions)
 $1^1/_2$ cups apple cider
 1/2 cup red wine vinegar
  1 package ($1^3/_4$ ounces) powdered
      fruit pectin
 $1^1/_2$ teaspoons either dried rosemary
      leaves **OR** dried thyme leaves,
      crushed
 1/2 teaspoon ground black pepper
 1/2 teaspoon olive oil
  4 cups granulated sugar
 3/4 cup firmly packed brown sugar

In a Dutch oven, combine onions, apple cider, red wine vinegar, pectin, rosemary **or** thyme, pepper, and olive oil over medium-high heat. Bring to a rolling boil. Add sugars. Stirring constantly, bring to a rolling boil again and boil 1 minute. Remove from heat; skim off foam. Spoon jam into heat-resistant jars; cover and cool to room temperature. Store in refrigerator.
Yield: about 6 cups jam

GIFT BASKET
(Shown on page 105)

You will need a basket, gold spray paint, excelsior, red raffia, gold cord, artificial berry pick, artificial greenery, hot glue gun, decorative-edge craft scissors, green card stock, gold paint pen, and a hole punch.

1. Spray paint basket gold; allow to dry. Line basket with excelsior.
2. For bow, form three loops in center of a length of raffia. Pinch loops together at center. Tie a length of cord around gathers to secure. Use cord to tie bow to handle. Tie cord ends into a bow. Insert berry pick and greenery under knot; glue to secure.
3. For tag, use craft scissors to cut a 2" x $3^1/_2$" piece of card stock. Use gold pen to write "Happy Holidays" on tag. Punch hole in tag. Use a length of raffia to tie tag to basket.

APRICOT CHEESE LOG
(Shown on page 105)

 1/2 cup finely chopped dried apricots
  5 tablespoons apricot brandy
  2 cups (8 ounces) shredded sharp
      Cheddar cheese
  4 ounces cream cheese, softened
 1/8 teaspoon dry mustard
 3/4 cup slivered almonds, toasted and
      coarsely chopped
      Crackers to serve

In a small bowl, combine apricots and brandy. Cover and let stand 1 hour.
In a medium bowl, combine Cheddar cheese, cream cheese, and dry mustard; beat about 3 minutes or until fluffy. Stir in apricot mixture. Cover and chill 1 hour.
Place cheese mixture on plastic wrap; shape into an 8-inch-long roll. Press almonds onto cheese roll. Wrap in plastic wrap. Store in refrigerator. Serve with crackers.
Yield: 1 cheese log (about $1^3/_4$ cups cheese)

THE TASTES OF CHRISTMAS

One of our favorite holiday traditions is gathering with special people to enjoy the tastes of the season. As part of this joyous celebration, we take pleasure in preparing an array of fabulous foods. In this delectable sampling of Yuletide delights, you'll find all the recipes you need, from scrumptious main dishes to decadent desserts. We've even made your planning easier with dishes you can make ahead for a formal feast or whip up in no time for a small get-together. So whether you make an entire meal or just choose a few favorite treats, you're sure to make the most of this festive time of year!

All Wrapped Up For Christmas

One of the most enjoyable elements of celebrating Christmas is opening our homes to friends and family. You'll have the menu all wrapped up when you choose from the delicious party recipes in this section — we've even included ways to "package" some of the foods in nifty ways! Guests will love mingling while dazzling their taste buds with scrumptious appetizers and mouth-watering drinks. So whip up a few of your favorite recipes, invite some friendly folks, and let the Yuletide festivities begin!

Spicy Cheddar Cheesecake with Apricot Chutney *(left)* is a savory selection that features a crust of tortilla chips and a hint of cumin for Mexican flair. Dainty finger food, Two-Tone Cucumber Sandwiches *(right)* are layered with cheesy, peppery filling and cool cucumber slices.

SPICY CHEDDAR CHEESECAKE WITH APRICOT CHUTNEY

Both the cheesecake and chutney can be made a day ahead.

CRUST
- 3/4 cup finely crushed tortilla chips
- 1/2 cup finely shredded sharp Cheddar cheese
- 2 tablespoons butter or margarine, melted
- 1/2 teaspoon ground cumin

FILLING
- 2 packages (8 ounces each) cream cheese, softened
- 2 eggs
- 1 cup (4 ounces) finely shredded sharp Cheddar cheese
- 1/3 cup finely chopped green onions
- 1 teaspoon Worcestershire sauce
- 1 teaspoon hot pepper sauce
- 1/2 teaspoon curry powder
- 1/4 teaspoon salt

CHUTNEY
- 1 tablespoon olive oil
- 2 tablespoons minced onion
- 1 clove garlic, minced
- 2 jars (12 ounces each) apricot preserves
- 1/4 cup orange juice
- 2 tablespoons apple cider vinegar

Preheat oven to 325 degrees. For crust, process tortilla chips, cheese, melted butter, and cumin in a food processor until blended. Press mixture into bottom of an ungreased 9-inch springform pan. Bake 15 minutes or until firm.

For filling, beat cream cheese and eggs in a medium bowl until well blended. Stir in Cheddar cheese, green onions, Worcestershire sauce, pepper sauce, curry powder, and salt. Spread mixture over crust. Bake 25 to 30 minutes or until center is set. Cool in pan. Remove sides of pan. Cover and chill at least 2 hours to let flavors blend.

For chutney, combine olive oil, onion, and garlic in a medium saucepan. Sauté over medium heat about 5 minutes or until vegetables are tender. Add preserves, orange juice, and vinegar. Stirring frequently, cook over medium heat until mixture comes to a boil. Reduce heat to medium low and simmer uncovered 17 minutes or until chutney thickens. Remove from heat and cool to room temperature. Store in an airtight container in refrigerator.

Chock-full of chopped tomatillos and avocado, Fresh Salsa Verde is a chunky treat that demands a second dip!

To serve, let chutney come to room temperature. Spoon about 1 cup chutney over chilled cheesecake. Cut into 20 small wedges; serve with remaining chutney.
Yield: 20 servings

TWO-TONE CUCUMBER SANDWICHES

Filling can be made a day ahead.

- 12 ounces cream cheese, softened
- 2 tablespoons finely chopped onion
- 1 teaspoon dried dill weed
- 1 teaspoon dried parsley flakes
- 1 teaspoon prepared horseradish
- 1/2 teaspoon salt
- 1/8 teaspoon hot pepper sauce
- 1 loaf (24 ounces) swirled wheat and white combination bread
- 1 medium cucumber, scored and thinly sliced
- 5 to 7 radishes, thinly sliced

In a medium bowl, beat cream cheese, onion, dill weed, parsley, horseradish, salt, and pepper sauce until well blended. Store in an airtight container in refrigerator until ready to serve.

To serve, let filling come to room temperature. Trim crusts from bread slices. Spread each slice with 1 tablespoon cream cheese mixture; cut each slice into 4 squares. Place a cucumber slice on half of bread squares; top with remaining bread squares, filling side down. Place 1 radish slice on a party pick and insert into each sandwich. Store in an airtight container in refrigerator.
Yield: about 2 1/2 dozen sandwiches

FRESH SALSA VERDE

- 1 pound fresh tomatillos, hulled and finely chopped
- 3/4 cup finely chopped onion
- 1/4 cup water
- 1/2 teaspoon salt
- 1 avocado, seeded, peeled, and chopped
- 1/4 cup chopped fresh cilantro
- 2 tablespoons freshly squeezed lime juice
- 2 to 3 cloves garlic, minced
- 1 small fresh jalapeño pepper, seeded and chopped
- 1/4 teaspoon ground black pepper
  Tortilla chips to serve

In a medium saucepan over medium heat, combine tomatillos, onion, water, and salt. Cover and cook about 15 minutes or until tomatillos are tender; drain. In a medium bowl, combine tomatillo mixture and remaining ingredients. Cover and chill 2 hours to let flavors blend. Serve with tortilla chips.
Yield: about 2 cups salsa

Give ordinary salsa a twist with Cherry Salsa *(left)*, a tart and tangy sensation. Plump with a seasoned mushroom filling, Savory Mushroom Pillows *(right)* are packaged in wonton wrappers and deep fried.

CHERRY SALSA

This salsa would also make a good accompaniment to grilled meat.

- 2 cans (15 ounces each) dark, sweet, pitted cherries in heavy syrup, drained and coarsely chopped
- 3 tablespoons chopped red onion
- 3 tablespoons chopped fresh basil leaves
- 3 tablespoons finely chopped green pepper
- 3 tablespoons honey
- 2 tablespoons finely chopped fresh jalapeño pepper
- 1 tablespoon freshly squeezed lemon juice
- 1 teaspoon grated lemon zest
- 1/2 teaspoon salt
  Tortilla chips to serve

In a medium bowl, combine cherries, onion, basil, green pepper, honey, jalapeño pepper, lemon juice, lemon zest, and salt. Cover and chill 2 hours to let flavors blend. Serve salsa with tortilla chips.
Yield: about 2 cups salsa

SAVORY MUSHROOM PILLOWS

This is another great make-ahead appetizer.

- 1 pound fresh mushrooms
- 3 tablespoons butter
- 1 tablespoon vegetable oil
- 1/4 cup finely chopped green onions
- 2 cloves garlic, minced
- 2 tablespoons dry white wine
- 1 teaspoon chopped fresh thyme leaves
- 1/2 teaspoon salt
- 1/2 teaspoon ground black pepper
- 4 ounces cream cheese, softened
- 1 package (12 ounces) wonton wrappers
  Vegetable oil

Process mushrooms in a food processor until finely chopped. Melt butter with 1 tablespoon oil in a large skillet over medium heat. Add mushrooms, green onions, and garlic; sauté about 20 minutes or until liquid from mushrooms evaporates. Stirring constantly, add wine and cook until liquid evaporates. Stir in thyme, salt, and pepper. Remove from heat and add cream cheese; stir until melted. Place 1 teaspoon mixture on lower half of each wonton wrapper. Brush edges with water; fold sides over filling. Fold lower edge of wrapper over filling and roll. Press edges to seal. Place, seam side down, on baking sheet. Cover and refrigerate until ready to serve.

To serve, deep fry appetizers in hot oil until browned, about 1 to 2 minutes. Drain on paper towels. Serve warm.
Yield: about 4 dozen appetizers

FALAFEL APPETIZERS WITH YOGURT MUSTARD SAUCE

SAUCE

- 2 containers (8 ounces each) plain yogurt
- 3 to 4 tablespoons Dijon-style mustard
- 2 teaspoons balsamic vinegar
- 2 teaspoons honey

APPETIZERS

- 2 cans (19 ounces each) chick peas, drained
- 1 egg, beaten
- 1/4 cup chopped onion
- 3 tablespoons chopped fresh parsley
- 1 1/2 tablespoons freshly squeezed lemon juice
- 4 cloves garlic, minced
- 3/4 teaspoon ground cumin
- 3/4 teaspoon salt
- 1/4 teaspoon ground black pepper
- 1/4 cup finely shredded carrots
- 1/4 cup purchased plain bread crumbs
- 2/3 cup sesame seeds, toasted

For sauce, combine yogurt, mustard, vinegar, and honey in a small bowl. Cover and chill until ready to serve.

For appetizers, process chick peas in a food processor just until puréed. Add egg, onion, parsley, lemon juice, garlic, cumin, salt, and pepper; pulse process until blended. Transfer mixture to a medium bowl. Stir in carrots and bread crumbs. Shape mixture into 1-inch balls. Place on an ungreased baking sheet; cover and chill 2 hours or until ready to serve.

To serve, preheat oven to 375 degrees. Roll falafel balls in toasted sesame seeds and return to baking sheet. Bake 18 to 22 minutes or until heated through. Serve warm with sauce.

Yield: about 6 dozen appetizers and 2 cups sauce

SPARKLING CHAMPAGNE PUNCH

- 2 bottles (750 ml each) champagne, chilled
- 1 bottle (750 ml) white wine, chilled
- 2 cups orange juice, chilled
- 2 cups cranberry juice, chilled
- 1/4 cup freshly squeezed lemon juice

Combine champagne, wine, orange juice, cranberry juice, and lemon juice in a 1-gallon container. Serve immediately.
Yield: about 13 1/2 cups punch

Easy-to-make Sparkling Champagne Punch will signal the beginning of the festivities. Toasted sesame seeds add texture to the delicate taste of Falafel Appetizers with Yogurt Mustard Sauce.

VIETNAMESE SPRING ROLLS WITH GARLIC-GINGER SAUCE

Spring rolls can be made ahead and refrigerated until ready to serve.

SPRING ROLLS
14 spring roll wrappers, 8½ inches in diameter (available at Oriental food stores)
2 cups coarsely chopped cooked shrimp (about 1 pound)
1 cup shredded carrots
1 cup shredded romaine lettuce
1 cup coarsely chopped fresh cilantro
1 tablespoon finely chopped fresh jalapeño pepper
1 clove garlic, minced
3 tablespoons freshly squeezed lime juice
1 tablespoon sesame oil
½ teaspoon salt

GARLIC-GINGER SAUCE
1 tablespoon cornstarch
½ cup low-sodium beef broth
3 cloves garlic, coarsely chopped
1 ounce fresh ginger, peeled and cut into small pieces (about 3 tablespoons)
¼ cup freshly squeezed lime juice
3 tablespoons fish sauce (available at Oriental food stores)
3 tablespoons sugar
1 tablespoon soy sauce

For spring rolls, place spring roll wrappers in a shallow dish; cover with cool water. In a medium bowl, combine shrimp, carrots, lettuce, cilantro, jalapeño pepper, and garlic. In a small bowl, combine lime juice, sesame oil, and salt; pour over shrimp mixture. For each spring roll, remove 1 wrapper from water and place on a paper towel. Pat top dry. Place ¼ cup filling in lower half of wrapper. Fold sides over filling. Fold lower edge of wrapper over filling and roll. Cover and chill until ready to serve.

For garlic-ginger sauce, dissolve cornstarch in beef broth in a small bowl. Process garlic and ginger in a small food processor until minced. In a small saucepan, combine garlic mixture, beef broth mixture, lime juice, fish sauce, sugar, and soy sauce. Stirring constantly, cook over medium heat about 10 minutes or until thickened; cool. Serve sauce at room temperature with spring rolls.
Yield: 14 spring rolls and 1 cup sauce

Seasoned Pita Wedges and zesty Sun-Dried Tomato Dip *(top)* make perfect partners for munching. *(Bottom)* Friends will love nibbling on robust Blue Cheese and Bacon-Stuffed Artichokes along with chilled Vietnamese Spring Rolls dipped in Garlic-Ginger Sauce.

BLUE CHEESE AND BACON-STUFFED ARTICHOKES

3 cans (14 ounces each) artichoke bottoms, drained
4 ounces cream cheese, softened
¼ cup mayonnaise
2 ounces blue cheese, crumbled
3 slices bacon, cooked and crumbled
1 teaspoon dried chives
1 tablespoon purchased plain bread crumbs

Preheat oven to 350 degrees. If necessary, trim bottoms of artichokes so they will sit flat. In a medium bowl, combine cream cheese, mayonnaise, and blue cheese; beat until well blended. Stir in bacon and chives. Spoon about ½ tablespoon cheese mixture onto each artichoke. Place on a lightly greased baking sheet. Cover and chill until ready to serve.

To serve, sprinkle stuffed artichokes with bread crumbs. Bake 24 to 28 minutes or until heated through and golden brown. Serve warm or at room temperature.
Yield: about 2½ dozen appetizers

SUN-DRIED TOMATO DIP

1 container (15 ounces) ricotta
    cheese
1 jar (8 ounces) oil-packed
    sun-dried tomatoes, drained and
    chopped
1/2 cup mayonnaise
1/4 cup finely chopped green onions
1 clove garlic, minced
1 tablespoon freshly squeezed lemon
    juice
1/4 teaspoon salt

In a medium bowl, combine ricotta
cheese, tomatoes, mayonnaise, green
onions, garlic, lemon juice, and salt. Stir
until well blended. Serve with Seasoned
Pita Wedges.
Yield: about 3 cups dip

SEASONED PITA WEDGES

*Thin pita bread makes crisper wedges than
thick bread.*

5 pita bread rounds
1/2 cup butter or margarine
2 teaspoons dried parsley flakes
1/2 teaspoon garlic salt
1/4 teaspoon ground black pepper

Cut each bread round in half to form
2 pockets. Split each pocket in half. Cut
each half into 3 wedges. Preheat broiler.
Place bread on an ungreased baking
sheet. In a small saucepan, melt butter
over medium heat. Stir in parsley, garlic
salt, and black pepper. Remove from
heat. Brush butter mixture over both sides
of bread. Watching closely, broil 4 to
6 minutes or until golden brown, turning
once about halfway through broiling time.
Serve warm.
Yield: 60 wedges

MAKE-AHEAD SAUCY RIBS

5 pounds pork loin back ribs
    Salt
    Ground black pepper
1 cup finely chopped onion
1 cup finely chopped green pepper
3 tablespoons vegetable oil
1 bottle (28 ounces) ketchup
1 1/2 cups firmly packed brown sugar
3/4 cup orange marmalade
3/4 cup apple cider vinegar
1 tablespoon hot pepper sauce
1 teaspoon salt
3/4 teaspoon ground black pepper

Because most of the preparation can be done the night before, Make-Ahead
Saucy Ribs are a great choice for holiday parties.

Preheat oven to 350 degrees. Place rib
racks in a single layer in foil-lined baking
pans. Sprinkle ribs with salt and pepper.
Cover with foil and bake 1 hour or until
fully cooked. Let cool.

While ribs are cooking, sauté onion
and green pepper in oil in a large
saucepan over medium heat until tender.
Stir in ketchup, brown sugar, marmalade,
vinegar, pepper sauce, 1 teaspoon salt,
and 3/4 teaspoon black pepper. Stirring
constantly, bring sauce to a simmer.
Reduce heat to medium low. Stirring
frequently, cook sauce 30 minutes
(mixture will be thick). Remove from heat
and let cool.

Cut racks into individual ribs. Transfer
to a heavy-duty resealable plastic bag.
Pour 2 cups sauce over ribs; refrigerate
overnight to let ribs marinate. Store
remaining sauce in an airtight container
in refrigerator.

To serve, preheat oven to 425 degrees.
Place ribs in foil-lined baking pans.
Spoon sauce from plastic bag over ribs.
Bake uncovered 1 hour or until sauce
cooks onto ribs, turning every 15 minutes
and basting with remaining sauce. Serve
warm.
Yield: about 3 dozen ribs

(Clockwise from left) Topped with toasted chopped walnuts, Nutty Blue Cheese Spread turns plain crackers into hearty appetizers. Sips of Hot Spiced Fruit Tea will tickle the taste buds with the inviting flavors of fruit juices and fresh ginger. As pleasing to the eye as they are to the palate, Green Olive and Jalapeño Roll-Ups add zest to the table.

NUTTY BLUE CHEESE SPREAD

- 1 package (8 ounces) cream cheese, softened
- 1 package (4 ounces) blue cheese, crumbled
- 2 tablespoons sour cream
- 1/4 teaspoon ground red pepper
- 1/4 cup finely chopped celery
- 1/4 cup finely chopped green onions
- 1 1/2 cups chopped walnuts, toasted, finely chopped, and divided
  Crackers to serve

Process cream cheese, blue cheese, sour cream, and red pepper in a food processor until smooth. Add celery, green onions, and 1 cup walnuts; process just until blended. Transfer to a 2 1/2-cup serving container. Cover with plastic wrap and chill 2 hours to let flavors blend.

To serve, bring cheese spread to room temperature. Sprinkle with remaining 1/2 cup walnuts. Serve with crackers.
Yield: about 2 1/4 cups cheese spread

GREEN OLIVE AND JALAPEÑO ROLL-UPS

- 1 package (8 ounces) cream cheese, softened
- 1/2 cup mayonnaise
- 1 cup sliced pimiento-stuffed olives, chopped
- 1/2 cup chopped pecans, toasted and finely chopped
- 1 1/2 tablespoons chopped pickled jalapeño pepper
- 4 flavored tortilla wraps, 12 inches in diameter (we used spinach-herb and tomato-basil flavors)

In a medium bowl, combine cream cheese and mayonnaise; beat until smooth. Add olives, pecans, and jalapeño pepper; stir until well blended. Spread about 1/2 cup mixture onto each tortilla. Tightly roll up tortillas and wrap in plastic wrap. Chill 2 hours. Cut into 1/2-inch slices.
Yield: about 7 1/2 dozen slices

HOT SPICED FRUIT TEA

- 1 bottle (64 ounces) apple juice
- 4 cups water
- 1 can (6 ounces) frozen lemonade concentrate, thawed
- 10 orange-spice tea bags
- 1 two-inch-long piece fresh ginger, peeled and thinly sliced
- 1/2 cup firmly packed brown sugar
  Lemon slices to serve

Combine apple juice, water, and lemonade concentrate in a Dutch oven. Add tea bags and ginger slices. Bring to a simmer over medium-high heat. Reduce heat to low; simmer 15 minutes. Remove tea bags and ginger. Stir in brown sugar. Simmer 10 minutes. Serve warm with lemon slices.
Yield: about 12 cups tea

HERBED PIMIENTO DIP

- 1 container (8 ounces) fat-free sour cream
- 4 ounces fat-free cream cheese, softened
- 1/2 cup fat-free mayonnaise
- 1 clove garlic, minced
- 1 jar (7 ounces) sliced pimientos, drained
- 1 tablespoon chopped fresh basil leaves
- 1 tablespoon chopped fresh oregano leaves
- 1 teaspoon lemon pepper
- 1/2 teaspoon salt
  Fresh vegetables to serve

Process sour cream, cream cheese, mayonnaise, and garlic in a food processor until smooth. Add pimientos, basil, oregano, lemon pepper, and salt. Pulse process until blended. Transfer to a serving bowl. Cover and refrigerate 2 hours to let flavors blend. Serve with vegetables.
Yield: about 2 1/2 cups dip

1 serving (1 tablespoon): 14.3 calories, 0.1 gram fat, 1.0 gram protein, 2.2 grams carbohydrate

CHEESY CRAB PUFFS

Puffs can be prepared ahead of time and chilled or frozen until time to bake.

- 1 can (6 ounces) crabmeat, drained
- 4 ounces cream cheese, softened
- 1 cup (4 ounces) shredded Swiss cheese
- 1/4 cup finely chopped red pepper (we used an equal amount of sweet and jalapeño peppers)
- 2 tablespoons finely chopped green onion
- 2 tablespoons purchased plain bread crumbs
- 1 teaspoon freshly squeezed lemon juice
- 1 teaspoon prepared horseradish
- 1 teaspoon Worcestershire sauce
- 1/2 teaspoon garlic salt
- 1/8 teaspoon ground red pepper
- 1 package (17 1/4 ounces) frozen puff pastry, thawed according to package directions

In a medium bowl, combine crabmeat, cream cheese, Swiss cheese, chopped red pepper, green onion, bread crumbs, lemon juice, horseradish, Worcestershire sauce, garlic salt, and ground red pepper; beat until well blended. On a lightly

Cheesy Crab Puffs *(top)* are wrapped in puff pastry and baked for a tummy-warming treat. For a refreshingly lighter snack, try dipping vegetable sticks into Herbed Pimiento Dip *(bottom)* made with fat-free ingredients.

floured surface, use a floured rolling pin to roll each pastry sheet into a 10-inch square. Cut pastry into 2-inch squares. Press a pastry square into each ungreased cup of a non-stick miniature muffin pan. Spoon 1 teaspoon crab mixture into center of each square.

(Pastries may be covered and chilled or frozen at this time.)
Preheat oven to 400 degrees. Bake 19 to 21 minutes or until golden brown. (If puffs were chilled, bake 22 to 24 minutes. If puffs were frozen, bake 25 to 27 minutes.) Serve warm.
Yield: about 4 dozen puffs

125

SWEET NIGHT BEFORE CHRISTMAS

*For generations, children have eagerly awaited the most magical night of the year —
Christmas Eve. Cater to their imaginations with heavenly delicacies that seem to be taken
straight from the lines of Clement Moore's famous poem. Character cookies iced to
perfection and candies that melt in your mouth create a storybook display to behold. With
goodies that look as delightful as they taste, this scrumptious section will have folks
young and old dreaming of a visit from old Saint Nick!*

Amish Sugar Cookies are easy-to-make treats! Using one basic recipe, you can vary the ingredients to create an
assortment of delicious cookies.

AMISH SUGAR COOKIES

Variations on basic cookie are listed below.

- 1/2 cup butter or margarine, softened
- 1 1/2 cups sugar
- 1/2 cup sour cream
- 2 eggs
- 1 1/2 teaspoons vanilla extract
- 2 cups all-purpose flour
- 1 teaspoon baking powder
- 1/4 teaspoon salt

Preheat oven to 375 degrees. In a large bowl, cream butter and sugar until fluffy. Add sour cream, eggs, and vanilla; beat until smooth. In a small bowl, combine flour, baking powder, and salt. Add dry ingredients to creamed mixture; stir until a soft dough forms. Drop teaspoonfuls of dough 2 inches apart onto a lightly greased baking sheet. Bake 8 to 10 minutes or until bottoms are lightly browned. Transfer cookies to a wire rack to cool. Store in an airtight container.
Yield: about 6 1/2 dozen cookies

Chocolate-Chocolate Chip Cookies: Make Amish Sugar Cookies, adding 2 ounces melted semisweet baking chocolate to butter and sour cream mixture. Add 1 cup semisweet chocolate mini chips to dough.

Cherry-Almond Cookies: Make Amish Sugar Cookies, using 1 teaspoon almond extract instead of vanilla extract. Add 3/4 cup finely chopped red candied cherries and 3/4 cup finely chopped, toasted slivered almonds to dough.

Lemon-Pecan Cookies: Make Amish Sugar Cookies, using 1 teaspoon lemon flavoring instead of vanilla extract. Add 1 cup finely chopped, toasted pecans to dough.

Spice-Walnut Cookies: Make Amish Sugar Cookies, adding 3/4 teaspoon ground cinnamon and 1/8 teaspoon ground cloves to dry ingredients. Add 1 cup chopped walnuts to dough.

FROSTED CANDY CANES

- 5 ounces vanilla candy coating, chopped
- 12 6-inch-long candy canes
  Coarse red decorating sugar
  White non-pareils

In a small saucepan, melt candy coating. Spoon coating over curved ends of candy canes. Sprinkle decorating sugar and non-pareils on coating before coating

These snacks look almost too good to eat! Easy Microwave Fudge whips up in a snap, and Frosted Candy Canes are made in two simple steps. Children and adults alike will have fun decorating Mice Cookies using peanut halves, shoestring licorice, and decorating sugar.

hardens. Place candy canes on waxed paper to let coating harden. Store in an airtight container.
Yield: 12 candy canes

EASY MICROWAVE FUDGE

- 1/2 cup butter or margarine
- 1 1/2 cups sugar
- 1 can (5 ounces) evaporated milk
- 2 cups miniature marshmallows
- 1 package (6 ounces) semisweet chocolate chips
- 1 teaspoon vanilla extract

(**Note:** This recipe was tested in a 700-watt microwave.) Line an 8-inch square baking pan with aluminum foil, extending foil over 2 sides of pan; grease foil. In a large microwave-safe bowl, microwave butter until melted. Stir in sugar and milk. Microwave on high power (100%) 8 minutes, stirring every 2 minutes. Add marshmallows, chocolate chips, and vanilla; stir until smooth. Pour mixture into prepared pan; chill 2 hours or until firm.

Use ends of foil to lift fudge from pan. Cut into 1-inch squares. Store in an airtight container in refrigerator.
Yield: about 4 dozen pieces fudge

MICE COOKIES

- 3/4 cup butter or margarine, softened
- 1/2 cup smooth peanut butter
- 1 cup firmly packed brown sugar
- 1 egg
- 1 teaspoon vanilla extract
- 2 1/2 cups all-purpose flour
- 1/3 cup peanuts
  Red shoestring licorice
  Black coarse decorating sugar

Preheat oven to 325 degrees. In a large bowl, cream butter, peanut butter, and brown sugar until fluffy. Add egg and vanilla; beat until smooth. Add flour to creamed mixture; stir until a soft dough forms. Shape dough into 1-inch balls. Pinch each ball to form a nose. Decorate each cookie using peanut halves for ears, small pieces of licorice for eyes, and a sugar crystal for nose. Use a toothpick to poke a hole in back of each cookie for tail. Transfer to an ungreased baking sheet. Bake 10 to 12 minutes or until bottoms are lightly browned. Transfer cookies to a wire rack. While cookies are warm, insert 2-inch-long pieces of licorice into holes for tails. Cool completely. Store in an airtight container.
Yield: about 4 1/2 dozen cookies

You won't find these stockings hanging by the chimney! Bright icings give Almond Stocking Cookies a glossy painted look. Apricot-Nut Balls are covered in tasty coatings of coconut, toasted almonds, and confectioners sugar.

ALMOND STOCKING COOKIES

COOKIES
- 1 can (8 ounces) almond paste, coarsely crumbled
- ³/₄ cup butter or margarine, softened
- ¹/₂ cup granulated sugar
- ¹/₂ cup confectioners sugar
- 1 egg
- 1 teaspoon almond extract
- 2¹/₄ cups all-purpose flour
- ¹/₄ teaspoon salt

ICING
- 5 cups confectioners sugar
- 5¹/₂ to 6¹/₂ tablespoons water
- 1¹/₂ teaspoons almond extract
  Red and green paste food coloring

Preheat oven to 350 degrees. For cookies, place almond paste in a large microwave-safe bowl. Microwave on high power (100%) 25 seconds or until paste softens. Add butter and sugars; cream until fluffy. Add egg and almond extract; beat until smooth. In a medium bowl, combine flour and salt. Add dry ingredients to creamed mixture; stir until a soft dough forms. On a lightly floured surface, use a floured rolling pin to roll out half of dough to ¹/₄-inch thickness. Use a 2 x 3¹/₄-inch stocking-shaped cookie cutter to cut out cookies. Transfer cookies to a lightly greased baking sheet. Bake 10 to 12 minutes or until bottoms are lightly browned. Transfer cookies to a wire rack to cool. Repeat with remaining dough.

For icing, combine confectioners sugar, water, and almond extract in a medium bowl; beat until smooth. Transfer icing into 3 small bowls; tint red and green, leaving remaining bowl white. Spoon icing into pastry bags fitted with small round tips. Outline "cuff" and fill in with white icing; let icing harden. Pipe "toe" and "heel" shapes on each cookie using red or green icing; let icing harden. Outline remainder of cookie and fill in with red or green icing; let icing harden. Using red or green icing and a very small round tip, pipe words on cuffs of stockings; let icing harden. Store in an airtight container.
Yield: about 2 dozen cookies

APRICOT-NUT BALLS

- 1 package (6 ounces) chopped dried apricots
- ¹/₂ cup apricot brandy
- 1¹/₃ cups slivered almonds, toasted, coarsely ground, and divided
- ¹/₂ cup light corn syrup
- ¹/₂ cup confectioners sugar, divided
- 1 package (11 ounces) vanilla wafers, finely crushed
- ¹/₂ cup flaked coconut

In a small bowl, combine apricot pieces and brandy. Cover and let stand 1 hour.

In a medium bowl, combine apricot mixture, 1 cup almonds, corn syrup, ¹/₄ cup confectioners sugar, and cookie crumbs. With greased hands, shape mixture into 1-inch balls. Roll one-third of balls in remaining ¹/₃ cup almonds, one-third in coconut, and one-third in remaining ¹/₄ cup confectioners sugar; transfer to waxed paper. Let stand 15 minutes; roll sugar-coated balls in confectioners sugar again. Store in an airtight container in refrigerator.
Yield: about 5 dozen candies

BEDTIME COOKIES

COOKIES
- ¹/₂ cup butter or margarine, softened
- ¹/₃ cup vegetable shortening
- 1 cup sugar
- ¹/₄ cup molasses
- 1 egg
- 1 teaspoon vanilla extract
- 3 cups all-purpose flour
- 1 teaspoon ground cinnamon
- ¹/₄ teaspoon salt

DECORATING ICING
- 2¹/₂ cups confectioners sugar
- 3 to 4 tablespoons water
- ¹/₂ teaspoon vanilla extract
  - Green, red, and yellow paste food coloring

GLAZE
- 3¹/₃ cups confectioners sugar
- 4 to 5 tablespoons water
- 1 teaspoon vanilla extract
  - Yellow paste food coloring

Preheat oven to 350 degrees. For cookies, cream butter, shortening, and sugar in a medium bowl until fluffy. Add molasses, egg, and vanilla; beat until smooth. In a another medium bowl, combine flour, cinnamon, and salt. Add dry ingredients to creamed mixture; stir until a soft dough forms. Divide dough in half. On a lightly floured surface, use a floured rolling pin to roll out half of dough to ¹/₈-inch thickness. Use a 2¹/₄ x 3¹/₂-inch boy-shaped cookie cutter to cut out cookies. Transfer to a greased baking sheet. Bake 5 to 7 minutes or until bottoms are lightly browned. Transfer cookies to a wire rack to cool. Repeat with remaining dough and use a 2¹/₄ x 3¹/₂-inch girl-shaped cookie cutter to cut out cookies.

For decorating icing, combine confectioners sugar, water, and vanilla in a medium bowl; stir until smooth. Transfer icing into 3 small bowls; tint green, red, and yellow. Spoon icing into pastry bags fitted with small round tips. Pipe green icing onto each boy cookie to outline pajamas. Pipe red icing onto each girl cookie to outline nightgown. Pipe yellow icing onto each cookie to outline hair. Cover pastry bag tips with plastic wrap. Let icing on cookies harden.

For glaze, combine confectioners sugar, water, and vanilla in a small bowl; stir until smooth (icing should be thin enough to flow easily). Transfer ¹/₂ cup glaze into a small bowl; tint yellow. Spoon white and yellow glazes into 2 pastry bags fitted with medium round

Dressed in icing pajamas, Bedtime Cookies make a great offering for old Saint Nick. For truly munchable morsels, try serving Fruity Brittle that features gumdrops surrounded by crunchy candy.

tips. Pipe yellow glaze onto cookies, filling in hair outlines. Pipe white glaze onto cookies, filling in pajama and nightgown outlines. Let glaze harden.

Using decorating icing, pipe green eyes and red mouths onto cookies. Pipe green stripes onto pajamas of boy cookies and red dots onto nightgowns of girl cookies. Let icing harden. Store in an airtight container.

Yield: about 3¹/₂ dozen cookies

FRUITY BRITTLE

- 1 cup chopped soft green and red fruit-flavored candy slices **or** small gumdrops
- 1¹/₂ cups sugar
- ¹/₂ cup light corn syrup
- ¹/₄ cup water
- 2 tablespoons butter or margarine
- ¹/₂ teaspoon salt
- 1 teaspoon baking soda

Line a baking sheet with aluminum foil; grease foil. Sprinkle candy in a 10 x 12-inch area on prepared baking sheet. Butter sides of a heavy medium saucepan. Combine sugar, corn syrup, and water in saucepan. Stirring constantly, cook over medium-low heat until sugar dissolves. Using a pastry brush dipped in hot water, wash down any sugar crystals on sides of pan. Attach a candy thermometer to pan, making sure thermometer does not touch bottom of pan. Increase heat to medium and bring to a boil. Cook, without stirring, until mixture reaches hard-crack stage (approximately 300 to 310 degrees) and turns light golden brown in color. Test about ¹/₂ teaspoon mixture in ice water. Mixture will form brittle threads in ice water and will remain brittle when removed from water. Remove from heat and add butter and salt; stir until butter melts. Add baking soda (mixture will foam); stir until soda dissolves. Pour mixture over candy. Cool completely. Break into pieces. Store in an airtight container.

Yield: about 1 pound, 5 ounces brittle

CHOCOLATE-DIPPED CHERRIES

  1 jar (10 ounces) maraschino cherries with stems
  2 ounces semisweet baking chocolate
  2 ounces chocolate candy coating

Drain cherries and pat dry with paper towels. Melt chocolate and candy coating in a small saucepan over low heat. Dip three-fourths of each cherry into melted chocolate. Place dipped cherries on a baking sheet lined with waxed paper. Chill until chocolate hardens. Place in candy cups and store in an airtight container in refrigerator.
Yield: about 2$\frac{1}{2}$ dozen cherries

SURPRISE OATMEAL MUFFINS

MUFFINS
  1 cup all-purpose flour
  $\frac{1}{2}$ cup firmly packed brown sugar
  2 teaspoons baking powder
  $\frac{1}{2}$ teaspoon salt
  $\frac{1}{4}$ teaspoon ground cinnamon
  1 cup quick-cooking oats
  1 cup milk
  $\frac{1}{4}$ cup vegetable oil
  1 egg, beaten
  $\frac{1}{3}$ cup plus 1 tablespoon seedless raspberry jam

ICING
  1 package (3 ounces) cream cheese, softened
  3 tablespoons butter or margarine, softened
  1$\frac{1}{2}$ cups confectioners sugar
  $\frac{1}{2}$ teaspoon vanilla extract

Preheat oven to 375 degrees. For muffins, combine first 5 ingredients in a medium bowl. Stir in oats. In a small bowl, combine milk, oil, and egg. Add milk mixture to dry ingredients; stir just until blended. Spoon 1 tablespoon batter into each greased cup of a miniature muffin pan. Drop $\frac{1}{2}$ teaspoonful jam into center of batter in each cup. Bake 14 to 16 minutes or until lightly browned on top. Cool in pan 5 minutes. Transfer muffins to a wire rack to cool completely.
For icing, beat cream cheese and butter in a small bowl until fluffy. Add confectioners sugar and vanilla; beat until smooth. Spoon icing into a pastry bag fitted with a large round tip. Pipe icing onto center of each muffin. Store in an airtight container in refrigerator.
Yield: about 2$\frac{1}{2}$ dozen muffins

(Clockwise from top) Perfect morning snacks, Surprise Oatmeal Muffins have secret fruity middles and rich cream cheese icing. Our Chocolate-Dipped Cherries are a cinch to make by dipping maraschino cherries into melted chocolate coating. No one will be able to eat just one of these chunky Fruitcake Bars, which boast lots of candied fruit and nuts.

FRUITCAKE BARS

- 1/4 cup frozen orange juice concentrate, thawed
- 1/3 cup honey
- 2 cups raisins
- 2/3 cup butter or margarine, softened
- 1/3 cup granulated sugar
- 1/3 cup firmly packed brown sugar
- 3 eggs
- 1 teaspoon vanilla extract
- 1 1/4 cups all-purpose flour
- 1 teaspoon ground cinnamon
- 1/2 teaspoon baking powder
- 1/4 teaspoon ground allspice
- 1/4 teaspoon salt
- 1 cup graham cracker crumbs
- 1 cup finely chopped pecans
- 1/2 cup flaked coconut
- 1 package (4 ounces) red candied cherries, chopped
- 1 package (4 ounces) green candied cherries, chopped
- 1 package (4 ounces) candied pineapple, chopped

Line a 10 1/2 x 15 1/2-inch jellyroll pan with aluminum foil, extending foil over ends of pan; grease foil. In a medium microwave-safe bowl, combine juice concentrate and honey. Cover and microwave on high power (100%) about 4 minutes or until liquid boils. Stir in raisins; cover and let stand 30 minutes.

Preheat oven to 350 degrees. In a medium bowl, cream butter and sugars until fluffy. Add eggs and vanilla; beat until smooth. In a small bowl, combine flour, cinnamon, baking powder, allspice, and salt. Add dry ingredients to creamed mixture; stir until well blended. Stir in raisin mixture, cracker crumbs, pecans, coconut, and candied fruit. Spread mixture into prepared pan. Bake 19 to 21 minutes or until a toothpick inserted in center of fruitcake comes out clean. Cool in pan.

Use ends of foil to lift fruitcake from pan. Use a serrated knife to cut fruitcake into 1 1/2 x 2-inch bars. Store in an airtight container.

Yield: about 4 dozen bars

PEANUT BUTTER CANDY BARS

CRUST

- 1 1/2 cups quick-cooking oats
- 1/2 cup firmly packed brown sugar
- 1/2 cup salted peanuts
- 1/4 cup butter or margarine, softened
- 3 tablespoons light corn syrup
- 2 tablespoons smooth peanut butter
- 1/2 teaspoon vanilla extract

Layered with a crunchy crust, a super rich filling, and a chewy, gooey topping, Peanut Butter Candy Bars are a triple treat!

FILLING

- 1 jar (7 ounces) marshmallow creme
- 2 cups sugar
- 1/2 cup water
- 1/2 cup light corn syrup
- 1/8 teaspoon salt
- 1/2 cup smooth peanut butter
- 1/2 teaspoon vanilla extract

TOPPING

- 1 package (14 ounces) caramels
- 2 tablespoons water
- 1/2 cup salted peanuts, coarsely ground
- 1/2 cup milk chocolate chips
- 4 ounces chocolate candy coating, chopped

Line a 10 1/2 x 15 1/2-inch jellyroll pan with aluminum foil, extending foil over ends of pan; grease foil. For crust, process oats, brown sugar, peanuts, butter, corn syrup, peanut butter, and vanilla in a large food processor. Press mixture into bottom of prepared pan.

For filling, spoon marshmallow creme into a large bowl; set aside. Butter sides of a heavy medium saucepan. Combine sugar, water, corn syrup, and salt in saucepan. Stirring constantly, cook over medium-low heat until sugar dissolves. Using a pastry brush dipped in hot water, wash down any sugar crystals on sides of pan. Attach a candy thermometer to pan, making sure thermometer does not touch bottom of pan. Increase heat to medium and bring to a boil. While mixture is cooking, microwave peanut butter in a small microwave-safe bowl until hot. Cook candy mixture, without stirring, until mixture reaches hard-ball stage (approximately 250 to 268 degrees). Test about 1/2 teaspoon mixture in ice water. Mixture will roll into a hard ball in ice water and will remain hard when removed from water; remove from heat. While beating with an electric mixer at medium speed, slowly pour candy mixture over marshmallow creme. Add peanut butter and vanilla; beat at high speed just until mixture holds its shape (about 3 minutes). Spread filling over crust.

For topping, combine caramels and water in a small microwave-safe bowl. Microwave on high power (100%) 3 minutes or until caramels melt, stirring after each minute. Stir in peanuts; spread caramel mixture over filling. In a small microwave-safe bowl, combine chocolate chips and candy coating. Microwave on medium-high power (80%) 2 minutes or until chocolate softens; stir until smooth. Spread chocolate over caramel mixture. Chill uncovered until firm enough to cut.

Use ends of foil to lift candy from pan. Cut into 1-inch squares. Store in an airtight container in refrigerator.

Yield: about 12 1/2 dozen candies

An eye-catching confection, this Crispy Popcorn Wreath is a tasty way to "ring" in the holidays! Shape the wreath in a ring mold, and then embellish it with tasty decorations like jelly roll-up candy "ribbon" and candied cherry "berries."

CRISPY POPCORN WREATH

    10 cups popped popcorn
        Vegetable cooking spray
    10 green candied cherries
     5 red candied cherries
     1 cup sugar
    3/4 cup water
    1/4 cup light corn syrup
    1/2 teaspoon white vinegar
    1/2 teaspoon salt
     1 teaspoon almond extract
        Red fruit-flavored roll-up candy
           (7/8-inch wide)

Place popcorn in a large bowl sprayed with cooking spray. Spray an 8-cup ring mold with cooking spray. Placing 2 green and 1 red cherry together, arrange cherries in 5 groups in bottom of mold. Butter sides of a heavy saucepan. Combine sugar, water, corn syrup, vinegar, and salt in saucepan. Stirring constantly, cook over medium-low heat until sugar dissolves. Using a pastry brush dipped in hot water, wash down any sugar crystals on sides of pan. Attach

candy thermometer to pan, making sure thermometer does not touch bottom of pan. Increase heat to medium and bring to a boil. Cook, without stirring, until mixture reaches soft-crack stage (approximately 270 to 290 degrees). Test about 1/2 teaspoon mixture in ice water. Mixture will form hard threads in ice water but will soften when removed from water. Remove from heat and stir in almond extract. Pour mixture over popcorn; stir until well coated. With lightly greased hands, press popcorn mixture into mold. Let cool.

Invert onto a serving plate. Decorate with roll-up candy "ribbon." Store in an airtight container.
Yield: about 10 servings

TINY REINDEER COOKIES

    3/4 cup butter or margarine, softened
    1/2 cup chopped pecans, toasted and
           finely ground
    1 1/2 cups confectioners sugar
     1 egg
     1 teaspoon vanilla-butter-nut
           flavoring
     2 cups all-purpose flour
    1/2 cup cocoa
    1/2 teaspoon salt

Preheat oven to 375 degrees. In a large bowl, cream butter, pecans, and confectioners sugar until fluffy. Add egg and vanilla-butter-nut flavoring; beat until smooth. In a small bowl, combine flour, cocoa, and salt. Add dry ingredients to creamed mixture; stir until a soft dough forms. Divide dough into fourths. Roll out one fourth of dough between sheets of plastic wrap to 1/4-inch thickness. Use a 2 1/2 x 3 1/4-inch reindeer-shaped cookie cutter to cut out cookies. Transfer to an ungreased baking sheet. Bake 5 to 7 minutes or until bottoms are lightly

browned. Cool cookies on baking sheet 2 minutes; transfer to a wire rack to cool completely. Repeat with remaining dough. Store in an airtight container.
Yield: about 3 dozen cookies

SAINT NICK COOKIES

These cookies require a cookie mold for their special look.

COOKIES
- 1 cup butter or margarine, softened
- 1 cup firmly packed brown sugar
- 1/2 cup granulated sugar
- 1 egg
- 2 teaspoons grated lemon zest
- 1 teaspoon vanilla extract
- 3 1/2 cups all-purpose flour
- 1/4 teaspoon ground cardamom
- 1/4 teaspoon salt
  Green, brown, ivory, red, and black paste food coloring

ICING
- 1/2 cup plus 2 tablespoons confectioners sugar
- 4 teaspoons milk

Preheat oven to 350 degrees. For cookies, cream butter and sugars in a large bowl until fluffy. Add egg, lemon zest, and vanilla; beat until smooth. In a medium bowl, combine flour, cardamom, and salt. Add dry ingredients to creamed mixture; stir until a soft dough forms. Press enough dough to fill a greased 4 x 6-inch Santa cookie mold (dough will be dry and crumbly, but will cling together when pressed). Loosen edges of dough with a knife. Invert mold and firmly rap edge on a wooden cutting board to release cookie. Place cookies on a greased baking sheet. Repeat with remaining dough. Bake 10 to 12 minutes or until edges are lightly browned. Cool cookies on baking sheet 5 minutes; transfer to a wire rack to cool.

To paint cookies, dilute a small amount of each food coloring with water, 1 drop at a time, in a small bowl. Referring to photo, use a small clean paintbrush to paint gift box and tree green; bag and tree trunk brown; cat and beak on bird ivory; bird, bow on gift box, hat, coat, cheeks, mouth, and nose on Santa red; and eye on bird, face on cat, eyes, glove, buttons, and boots on Santa black.

For icing, combine confectioners sugar and milk in a small bowl; stir until smooth. Use a clean paintbrush to brush white icing on beard, mustache, eyebrows, and trim on coat and hat. Let icing harden. Store in an airtight container.
Yield: about 10 cookies

Good old Santa Claus would never make his rounds without his eight tiny reindeer! Delicately painted with food coloring, our Saint Nick Cookies are little works of art. Tiny Reindeer Cookies lend a subtle chocolate flavor to the yummy cookie combination.

CANDLELIGHT CREOLE DINNER

Deep in the heart of the Delta lies a tradition of cooking passed down through generations of French Creole families. Seafood, vegetables, and robust sauces highlight the recipes that have made the Louisiana bayou famous. You can share this zesty style when you create a Yuletide feast using foods from this mouth-watering menu. Begin with spicy fried oysters or shrimp salad followed by a dish of grillades and grits to satisfy hearty appetites. From creamy soup to praline-covered cake, entice your guests with scrumptious foods from this feisty region of the South. Laissez le bon temps rouler (*Let the good times roll*)!

(*From left*) A rich concoction for quenching the thirst, Milk Punch with Bourbon (*in glass*) is a perky party potable. Toast wedges topped with tart and spicy Tapenade make scrumptious holiday appetizers. Fried Oysters with Spicy Tartar Sauce bring New Orleans flair to the table, and hearty stuffed Sausage-Cheese Bread is almost a meal in itself.

MILK PUNCH WITH BOURBON

6 cups milk
3 cups whipping cream
1 cup superfine sugar
3 tablespoons vanilla extract
3/4 cup bourbon
Freshly grated nutmeg to serve

In a 4-quart container, combine milk, whipping cream, superfine sugar, and vanilla; stir until sugar dissolves. Stir in bourbon. Cover and store in refrigerator about 2 hours or until chilled.

To serve, garnish individual servings with nutmeg.
Yield: about 11 cups punch

FRIED OYSTERS WITH SPICY TARTAR SAUCE

SPICY TARTAR SAUCE
3/4 cup mayonnaise
3 tablespoons Dijon-style mustard
1 tablespoon finely chopped onion
1 tablespoon finely chopped fresh parsley
1 tablespoon drained capers
1 teaspoon freshly squeezed lemon juice
1/2 teaspoon hot pepper sauce

OYSTERS
1 egg
3 tablespoons milk
3/4 cup yellow cornmeal
1/4 cup all-purpose flour
1/2 teaspoon salt
1/4 teaspoon ground black pepper
1/8 teaspoon ground red pepper
3 dozen shucked oysters **or** 2 containers (10 ounces each) fresh oysters, drained
Vegetable oil

For spicy tartar sauce, combine mayonnaise, Dijon mustard, onion, parsley, capers, lemon juice, and pepper sauce in a small bowl. Cover and chill 2 hours to let flavors blend.

For oysters, beat egg and milk in a small bowl. In another small bowl, combine cornmeal, flour, salt, and peppers. Dip each oyster into milk mixture, then into cornmeal mixture. Deep fry in hot oil until golden brown. Transfer to paper towels to drain. Serve warm with sauce.
Yield: about 3 dozen oysters and 1 cup sauce

Perfect for the salad course, Shrimp Rémoulade (*recipe on page 136*) is a light delicacy featuring chilled shrimp and thin vegetable strips topped with a deliciously tangy sauce.

TAPENADE

2 jars (10 ounces each) Kalamata olives, pitted
1 jar (3 1/4 ounces) capers, drained
1 can (6 ounces) oil-packed tuna
3 tablespoons olive oil
1 teaspoon freshly squeezed lemon juice
1 clove garlic, chopped
1/4 teaspoon red pepper flakes
Toasted white cocktail bread

Pulse process olives, capers, undrained tuna, olive oil, lemon juice, garlic, and red pepper flakes in a food processor just until mixture forms a coarse paste. Serve with toast.
Yield: about 3 cups spread

SAUSAGE-CHEESE BREAD

3 to 3 1/2 cups all-purpose flour, divided
2 packages dry yeast
1 tablespoon sugar
1 teaspoon salt
1/2 teaspoon dry mustard
1/4 teaspoon garlic powder
1/4 teaspoon onion powder
1/8 teaspoon ground red pepper
1/2 cup butter or margarine
1 cup milk
2 cups (8 ounces) shredded sharp Cheddar cheese
Vegetable cooking spray
8 ounces andouille sausage (or other spicy sausage), browned, drained, and crumbled
1 egg white, beaten

In a large bowl, combine 2 cups flour, yeast, sugar, salt, dry mustard, garlic powder, onion powder, and red pepper. In a small saucepan, combine butter and milk over medium-low heat; stir until butter melts. Pour milk mixture into flour mixture; stir until well blended. Gradually stir in 1 cup flour and cheese. Turn onto a lightly floured surface. Knead about 5 minutes or until dough becomes smooth and elastic, using additional flour as necessary. Place in a large bowl sprayed with cooking spray, turning once to coat top of dough. Cover and let rise in a warm place (80 to 85 degrees) 1 1/2 hours or until doubled in size.

(Continued on page 136)

Turn dough onto a lightly floured surface and punch down. Divide dough into thirds. With a lightly floured rolling pin, roll one third of dough into a 6 x 15-inch rectangle. Sprinkle one third of sausage lengthwise down center of dough. Beginning at 1 long edge, roll up dough jellyroll style. Pinch seam to seal. Repeat with remaining dough and sausage. On a lightly greased baking sheet, braid ropes with seam sides down. Pinch ends of ropes together to seal; turn ends under. Spray top of dough with cooking spray, cover, and let rise in a warm place 45 minutes or until doubled in size.

Preheat oven to 350 degrees. Brush egg white over dough. Bake 30 to 35 minutes or until bread is golden brown and sounds hollow when tapped. Cover with aluminum foil if top browns too quickly. Serve warm or transfer to a wire rack to cool completely. Cut into $^1/_2$-inch slices, then cut each slice in half.
Yield: about 2 dozen servings

SHRIMP RÉMOULADE

(Shown on page 135)

2 cups mayonnaise
1 cup finely chopped green onions
$^1/_2$ cup finely chopped celery
$^1/_4$ cup chopped fresh parsley
2 tablespoons Creole mustard
1 tablespoon freshly squeezed lemon juice
1 tablespoon finely chopped sour pickles
1 tablespoon drained capers
2 cloves garlic, minced
1 teaspoon paprika
1 teaspoon prepared horseradish
1 teaspoon anchovy paste
$^1/_2$ teaspoon finely chopped fresh tarragon leaves
Romaine lettuce, shredded
1$^1/_4$ pounds medium shrimp, cooked, shelled (leaving tails on), deveined, and chilled
1 sweet red pepper, sliced
1 green pepper, sliced

In a medium bowl, combine mayonnaise, green onions, celery, parsley, Creole mustard, lemon juice, pickles, capers, garlic, paprika, horseradish, anchovy paste, and tarragon; stir until well blended. Cover and chill overnight.

To serve, place lettuce on 8 serving plates. Top with shrimp and pepper slices. Spoon rémoulade sauce onto each salad.
Yield: 8 servings

Creamy Corn Muffins baked in mini muffin pans are bite-size munchies for accompanying steaming bowls of thick Cream of Artichoke Soup. Both recipes require little preparation, so you can take time to enjoy them with your guests.

CREAM OF ARTICHOKE SOUP

2 tablespoons olive oil
2 tablespoons butter
1 cup chopped onion
$^1/_2$ cup chopped celery
2 cans (14$^1/_2$ ounces each) chicken broth
2 cans (14 ounces each) artichoke hearts, drained and chopped
1 large carrot, sliced
2 tablespoons freshly squeezed lemon juice
$^1/_2$ teaspoon salt
$^1/_2$ teaspoon ground white pepper
1 cup half and half
$^1/_4$ cup freshly grated Parmesan cheese
Celery leaves to garnish

In a Dutch oven, combine olive oil and butter over medium heat; stir until butter melts. Sauté onion and celery in oil mixture until onion is translucent. Stir in chicken broth, artichokes, carrot, lemon juice, salt, and white pepper. Cover and cook about 30 minutes or until vegetables are tender. Remove from heat. Purée vegetables in batches in a food processor. Return to Dutch oven. Stir in half and half and cheese. Serve warm or store in an airtight container in refrigerator.

To reheat, cook over medium-low heat uncovered about 20 minutes or until heated through, stirring frequently. Garnish individual servings with celery leaves.
Yield: about 8 cups soup

CREAMY CORN MUFFINS

1 cup yellow cornmeal
1 cup all-purpose flour
2 tablespoons sugar
1 tablespoon baking powder
$^3/_4$ teaspoon salt
$^1/_2$ teaspoon baking soda
1 can (8$^1/_2$ ounces) cream-style corn
1 cup sour cream
$^1/_4$ cup butter or margarine, melted
1 egg

Preheat oven to 375 degrees. In a medium bowl, combine cornmeal, flour, sugar, baking powder, salt, and baking soda. In a small bowl, beat corn, sour cream, melted butter, and egg until well blended. Add to dry ingredients; stir just until blended. Spoon batter into lightly greased miniature muffin pans. Bake 16 to 18 minutes or until tops are lightly browned. Serve warm.
Yield: about 4 dozen muffins

GRILLADES AND GRITS

 2 pounds beef or veal round roast
  (we used eye of round)
 1/2 cup all-purpose flour
 2 tablespoons salt
 1 tablespoon ground black pepper
 1/2 teaspoon ground red pepper
  Vegetable oil
 1 cup finely chopped white onion
 1/2 cup finely chopped green onions
 1 cup finely chopped green pepper
 1 cup finely chopped celery
 2 cloves garlic, minced
 1 can (14 1/2 ounces) diced tomatoes
 1 can (8 ounces) tomato sauce
 1 tablespoon Worcestershire sauce
 1 bay leaf
 4 cups cooked grits

Cut meat into 8 slices. Pound each piece to about 1/2-inch thickness. In a medium bowl, combine flour, salt, black pepper, and red pepper. Dredge pieces of meat in flour mixture. In a large skillet over medium-high heat, brown both sides of meat in oil. Transfer meat to a warm plate. Reserving about 3 tablespoons oil in skillet, sauté onions, green pepper, celery, and garlic until vegetables are tender. Add undrained tomatoes, tomato sauce, Worcestershire sauce, and bay leaf; bring to a simmer. Return meat to skillet. Reduce heat to low. Cover and simmer about 1 hour or until meat is tender, turning meat occasionally. Serve with hot grits.
Yield: 8 servings

RATATOUILLE

This dish can be made ahead and reheated.

 10 slices bacon
 1 medium eggplant, peeled and
  cubed
 2 unpeeled zucchini, cubed
 2 green peppers, chopped
 1 cup finely chopped onion
 2 cloves garlic, minced
 2 cans (14 1/2 ounces each) diced
  tomatoes
 1 package (10 ounces) frozen sliced
  okra, thawed
 3 tablespoons balsamic vinegar
 2 tablespoons finely chopped fresh
  parsley
 1 teaspoon salt
 1/2 teaspoon dried marjoram leaves
 1/2 teaspoon dried thyme leaves
 1/4 teaspoon ground black pepper

Cook bacon in a Dutch oven until crisp. Drain and crumble bacon; set

Packed with flavor, Ratatouille (*top*) combines vegetables and herbs for a tasty make-ahead side dish. Smothered in a robust red gravy, meaty Grillades and Grits (*bottom*) are mouth-watering Creole fare.

aside. Reserving 2 tablespoons drippings in pan, sauté eggplant, zucchini, green peppers, onion, and garlic over medium heat until vegetables are tender. Add undrained tomatoes, okra, vinegar, parsley, salt, marjoram, thyme, and black pepper. Cover and cook 20 minutes or until vegetables are tender, stirring frequently. Transfer to a serving dish. Sprinkle bacon over vegetables. Serve warm.
Yield: about 18 servings

CHEESE-STUFFED MIRLITONS

Mirlitons, also known as chayotes, are members of the squash family.

- 4 mirlitons (about 2½ pounds)
- 2 teaspoons plus ½ teaspoon salt, divided
- 2¼ cups fresh bread crumbs, divided
- ½ cup freshly grated Parmesan cheese, divided
- ¼ cup finely chopped green onions
- 1 egg
- 2 tablespoons chopped fresh parsley, divided
- 1 to 2 cloves garlic, minced
- ⅛ teaspoon ground black pepper
- ⅛ teaspoon ground red pepper
- 3 tablespoons butter or margarine, melted

Cut mirlitons in half lengthwise. Place in a large Dutch oven; cover with water and add 2 teaspoons salt. Bring to a boil over medium-high heat. Cover and reduce heat to medium low. Simmer until vegetables are barely tender (about 20 minutes). Drain mirlitons and cool.

Preheat oven to 350 degrees. Scoop seeds from mirlitons and discard. Scoop pulp into a medium bowl, leaving about a ⅛-inch-thick shell. Stir 2 cups bread crumbs, ¼ cup cheese, green onions, egg, 1 tablespoon parsley, garlic, peppers, and remaining ½ teaspoon salt into pulp. Spoon mixture into each shell. Place in a greased 9 x 13-inch baking dish. In a small bowl, combine remaining ¼ cup bread crumbs, ¼ cup cheese, and remaining 1 tablespoon parsley; sprinkle over squash. Drizzle with melted butter. Bake 45 minutes or until tops are golden brown. Serve warm.
Yield: 8 servings

CREAMED SPINACH

- ¼ cup butter or margarine
- 1 clove garlic, cut in half
- 6 tablespoons all-purpose flour
- 2¼ cups hot whipping cream
- ¾ teaspoon salt
- ¼ teaspoon ground white pepper
- 2 bags (10 ounces each) fresh spinach, stemmed and coarsely chopped
- ½ cup freshly grated Parmesan cheese

In a large skillet, melt butter over medium heat. Add garlic and sauté until garlic starts to brown; remove garlic.

With a scrumptious topping of bread crumbs and Parmesan cheese baked to a golden brown, Cheese-Stuffed Mirlitons (*bottom*) are a warm addition to the holiday table. Folks will want second helpings of quick-to-fix Creamed Spinach (*top*) seasoned with fresh garlic and Parmesan cheese.

Stirring constantly, add flour; stir until mixture is smooth. Cook 2 minutes. Stir in hot whipping cream, salt, and white pepper. Stirring constantly, bring to a boil and cook 2 minutes. Gradually stir in spinach. Reduce heat to medium low. Stirring frequently, cover and cook about 10 minutes or until spinach is tender. Stir in cheese. Serve warm.
Yield: about 9 servings

What would the holidays be without dessert! Our Sweet Potato Pie with Marshmallow Meringue puts a new twist on an old favorite. Top off a delicious meal with cups of spicy Café Brûlot, which is prepared by pouring strong coffee into a flaming mixture of spices and brandy.

SWEET POTATO PIE WITH MARSHMALLOW MERINGUE

Spoon meringue onto hot pie for best results.

PIE
- 1 can (29 ounces) sweet potatoes in syrup, drained and mashed
- 1 cup firmly packed brown sugar
- 2 tablespoons butter or margarine, softened
- 3 egg yolks
- 1 teaspoon pumpkin pie spice
- 1 teaspoon vanilla extract
- 1/4 teaspoon salt
- 1 can (5 ounces) evaporated milk
- 1 unbaked 9-inch deep-dish pie crust

MERINGUE
- 1/2 cup water
- 2 tablespoons sugar
- 1 tablespoon cornstarch
- 1/8 teaspoon salt
- 3 egg whites
- 1/4 teaspoon cream of tartar
- 1 jar (7 ounces) marshmallow creme
- 1/2 teaspoon vanilla extract

Preheat oven to 400 degrees. For pie, combine sweet potatoes, brown sugar, butter, egg yolks, pumpkin pie spice, vanilla, and salt in a medium bowl; beat until well blended. Stir in evaporated milk. Pour mixture into crust. Bake 10 minutes. Reduce heat to 350 degrees. Bake 40 minutes or until center is almost set and edges are cracked and lightly browned.

About 25 minutes after placing pie in oven, combine water, sugar, cornstarch, and salt in a small saucepan for meringue. Stirring constantly, cook over medium heat about 5 minutes or until mixture is clear. Transfer to a heatproof bowl. Cool about 15 minutes.

In a medium bowl, beat egg whites and cream of tartar until foamy. Add cornstarch mixture; beat until well blended. Gradually add marshmallow creme and vanilla; beat until soft peaks form. Top hot pie with meringue, sealing edges to crust; return pie to oven. Bake 12 to 15 minutes or until meringue is lightly browned. Let stand 30 minutes; serve warm.

Yield: about 8 servings

CAFÉ BRÛLOT

Use caution when igniting mixture.

- Shaved zest from half of an orange
- Shaved zest from half of a lemon
- 6 whole cloves
- 6 whole allspice
- 2 teaspoons superfine sugar
- 1/2 cup brandy
- 1 tablespoon Curaçao liqueur
- 4 cups hot strongly brewed coffee

Combine orange zest, lemon zest, cloves, allspice, and superfine sugar in a chafing dish over a heat source. Add brandy and liqueur; stir until sugar dissolves. As mixture begins to simmer, use a ladle to remove a small amount of brandy mixture. Ignite mixture in ladle and return to remaining mixture (flame will spread over surface). Slowly pour in coffee, stirring until flame goes out. Serve immediately.

Yield: about 4 cups coffee

Decorated with icing curlicues and an elegant monogram, French Quarter Cake is a dark, sweet ending to your holiday meal. Three layers of decadent cake are separated by an espresso-flavored chocolate filling, capturing the unique flavor of Bourbon Street.

FRENCH QUARTER CAKE

CAKE
- 1 1/2 cups all-purpose flour
- 1 1/4 cups sugar
- 3 tablespoons cocoa
- 2 teaspoons baking soda
- 1/2 teaspoon salt
- 4 eggs
- 1/2 cup buttermilk
- 1/2 cup coffee-flavored liqueur
- 1/3 cup vegetable oil
- 1 teaspoon vanilla extract
- 2 packages (3 ounces each) cream cheese, softened
- 6 ounces semisweet baking chocolate, melted

FILLING
- 1/2 cup whipping cream
- 2 teaspoons instant espresso powder
- 2 ounces semisweet baking chocolate, finely chopped

ICING
- 3 cups confectioners sugar
- 2/3 cup butter or margarine, softened
- 3 tablespoons cocoa
- 2 to 3 tablespoons milk
- 1 teaspoon vanilla extract

DECORATING ICING
- 2 cups confectioners sugar
- 2 tablespoons plus 1 teaspoon cocoa, divided
- 3 to 4 tablespoons coffee-flavored liqueur
- 1 teaspoon vanilla extract

Preheat oven to 350 degrees. For cake, grease three 8-inch round cake pans. Line bottoms with waxed paper; grease waxed paper. In a large bowl, combine flour, sugar, cocoa, baking soda, and salt. In a medium bowl, whisk eggs, buttermilk, liqueur, oil, and vanilla.

Add egg mixture to dry ingredients; stir until well blended. In a medium bowl, beat cream cheese and chocolate until well blended. Beat cream cheese mixture into batter. Pour batter into prepared pans. Bake 18 to 23 minutes or until a toothpick inserted in center of cake comes out clean. Cool in pans 10 minutes; remove from pans and cool completely on a wire rack.

For filling, combine whipping cream and espresso powder in a small saucepan. Bring to a boil over medium-high heat; pour mixture into a small bowl. Add chocolate; stir until smooth. Chill 10 minutes or until chocolate is cool but not set. Beat chocolate mixture until thickened (about 5 minutes). Spread filling between cake layers. Cover cake and chill 15 minutes or until filling is set.

For icing, combine confectioners sugar, butter, cocoa, milk, and vanilla in a large bowl; beat until smooth. Spread icing on top and sides of cake.

For decorating icing, combine confectioners sugar, 2 tablespoons cocoa, liqueur, and vanilla in a medium bowl; stir until smooth. Spoon icing into a pastry bag fitted with a small round tip. Using a toothpick, mark a 4-inch-diameter circle at center top of cake. Beginning at edge of circle, pipe connecting swirls onto top and sides of cake. Fill in circle with decorating icing. Pipe a small bead border around circle and top edge of cake. Allow icing to harden.

Transfer remaining decorating icing to a small bowl. Add remaining 1 teaspoon cocoa to icing to darken; stir until smooth. Return icing to pastry bag. Pipe desired initial in center of cake. Store in an airtight container in refrigerator. Serve at room temperature.

Yield: about 16 servings

Finish the feast with slices of Praline Angel Food Cake, a heavenly combination of airy cake covered with a crunchy praline topping.

PRALINE ANGEL FOOD CAKE

CAKE
- 10 egg whites
- 1¹/₂ teaspoons cream of tartar
- 1 teaspoon salt
- 1 teaspoon vanilla extract
- 1 teaspoon almond extract
- 2 cups firmly packed brown sugar, sifted and divided
- 1¹/₄ cups sifted cake flour
- 1 cup almond brickle chips

PRALINE TOPPING
- 1 cup firmly packed brown sugar
- 1¹/₂ tablespoons dark corn syrup
- 1 tablespoon water
- 1 tablespoon butter or margarine
- ¹/₂ teaspoon vanilla extract
- ¹/₂ teaspoon almond extract
- ¹/₂ cup almond brickle chips

Preheat oven to 350 degrees. For cake, beat egg whites in a large bowl until foamy. Add cream of tartar and salt; beat until soft peaks form. Add extracts. Gradually adding 1 cup brown sugar, beat until stiff peaks form. Sift remaining 1 cup brown sugar and cake flour over egg whites; fold into mixture. Fold in brickle chips. Pour into an ungreased 10-inch tube pan with a removable bottom. Bake 44 to 48 minutes or until top is golden brown. Invert pan; cool completely. Transfer cake to a serving plate.

For praline topping, butter sides of a heavy small saucepan. Combine brown sugar, corn syrup, water, and butter in saucepan. Stirring constantly, cook over medium-low heat until sugar dissolves. Using a pastry brush dipped in hot water, wash down any sugar crystals on sides of pan. Bring topping to a boil over medium heat; boil, without stirring, 3 minutes. Remove from heat; cool 5 minutes. Stir in extracts and brickle chips. Quickly pour glaze over cake. Let glaze harden.

Yield: about 16 servings

Cardinal Confections

The exquisite cardinal is a sure sign that winter — and Christmastime — is near. Their vibrant red feathers stand out against the natural backdrop of snowy fields and evergreens that define the most festive of all seasons. Bring these striking colors to your table with delightful desserts that pay tribute to this beautiful creature.

What a fun and tasty conversation piece for your holiday home! Using corn nuts, dried cranberries, cinnamon sticks, and popcorn, you can decorate this rustic Gingerbread Birdhouse that's edible when the cinnamon sticks are removed.

GINGERBREAD BIRDHOUSE

GINGERBREAD

- 1/2 cup butter or margarine, softened
- 1/3 cup firmly packed brown sugar
- 1/4 cup granulated sugar
- 2 eggs
- 1/3 cup dark corn syrup
- 1/4 cup molasses
- 4 to 4 1/4 cups all-purpose flour
- 1 teaspoon baking soda
- 1/2 teaspoon salt
- 1/2 teaspoon **each** ground allspice, ground cinnamon, ground cloves, and ground ginger
- 1 1 1/4-inch-long cinnamon stick

ICING AND DECORATIONS

- 1 1/2 tablespoons meringue powder
- 2 cups confectioners sugar
- 2 to 3 tablespoons water
  Brown paste food coloring
- 1 package (5 ounces) corn nuts
  Sweetened dried cranberries
- 3 cinnamon sticks, 1 about 7 1/2 inches long and 2 about 3 1/2 inches long
  Shredded toasted coconut
  Popped popcorn

For gingerbread, cream butter and sugars in a large bowl until fluffy. Add eggs, corn syrup, and molasses. Beat with an electric mixer until smooth. Sift flour, baking soda, salt, and ground spices into another large bowl. Stir dry ingredients into creamed mixture. Knead until a stiff dough forms. On a lightly floured surface, use a floured rolling pin to roll out dough to an 11 x 20-inch rectangle (about 1/4-inch thick). Cut the following pieces from dough: two 4 1/2 x 6 1/2-inch pieces for front and back, two 4 1/2 x 7 1/2-inch pieces for roof, and two 4 x 5-inch pieces for sides. Place all pieces on greased baking sheets.

Preheat oven to 325 degrees. On front piece, refer to **Fig. 1** and use a knife to trim into a house shape; use a 1 3/8-inch-diameter cookie cutter to cut a hole 2 inches from top. Remove scraps. Repeat for back piece, omitting hole.

Fig. 1

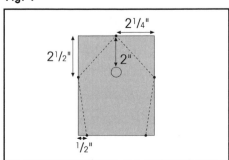

Glossy iced Cardinal Cookies *(recipe on page 144)* make an eye-catching holiday snack. Serve a plate of the delicious confections with a cup of hot Cherry-Berry Cider for a homey Yuletide treat.

For perch, press 1 end of cinnamon stick into front piece under hole. Bake gingerbread 10 to 15 minutes or until firm. Cool pieces on baking sheets 5 minutes; transfer to a wire rack to cool completely.

For icing, beat meringue powder, confectioners sugar, and water in a medium bowl at high speed of electric mixer 7 to 10 minutes or until stiff. Tint icing brown. Spoon half of icing into a pastry bag fitted with a medium round tip (refill bag as needed).

To assemble house, pipe icing along 1 short edge of 1 side piece; press onto back piece. Hold or prop pieces in place until icing begins to harden. Repeat for remaining side piece. Pipe icing along remaining short edge of each side piece; press front onto sides. Pipe icing along top edges of front and back pieces; center and press roof pieces into place.

For decorations, begin at 1 short edge of roof and pipe a line of icing from top to bottom of roof. Beginning at bottom of roof, press corn nuts into icing, overlapping nuts slightly. Repeat until roof is covered. Pipe icing along front edge of roof; press cranberries into icing. Repeat for back edge. Pipe icing along peak of roof; press 7 1/2-inch cinnamon stick into

icing. Pipe icing onto front piece close to roof; press 3 1/2-inch cinnamon sticks into icing. Pipe icing along inside bottom edge of hole; press coconut into icing. Place birdhouse on a board. Scatter popcorn and coconut around house.
Yield: one 7 1/2-inch-wide x 7 1/4-inch-high birdhouse

CHERRY-BERRY CIDER

- 1 package (12 ounces) frozen whole blackberries
- 1 package (12 ounces) frozen whole dark sweet cherries
- 3 cinnamon sticks
- 2 teaspoons whole allspice
- 1 gallon apple cider
  Cinnamon sticks to serve

In a Dutch oven, combine blackberries, cherries, 3 cinnamon sticks, and allspice. Add apple cider. Bring to a simmer over medium-high heat. Use a potato masher to mash fruit. Reduce heat to medium; cover and simmer 30 minutes. Strain mixture and serve warm with cinnamon sticks.
Yield: about 16 1/2 cups cider

CARDINAL COOKIES

(Shown on page 143)

COOKIES

- 3/4 cup butter or margarine, softened
- 1/2 cup granulated sugar
- 1/4 cup confectioners sugar
- 1 egg
- 1 egg yolk
- 2 teaspoons grated lemon zest
- 2 1/2 cups all-purpose flour
- 2/3 cup slivered almonds, toasted and finely ground

ICING

- 6 2/3 cups confectioners sugar
- 1/2 cup water
- 1 tablespoon light corn syrup
- 1 teaspoon almond extract
  Black, yellow, and red paste food coloring

Preheat oven to 350 degrees. Trace bird and wing patterns, page 145, separately onto stencil plastic; cut out. For cookies, cream butter and sugars in a large bowl until fluffy. Add egg, egg yolk, and lemon zest; beat until smooth. In a medium bowl, combine flour and almonds. Add dry ingredients to creamed mixture; stir until a soft dough forms. Divide dough in half. On a lightly floured surface, use a floured rolling pin to roll out half of dough to 1/8-inch thickness. Use patterns to cut out cookies. Transfer to a greased baking sheet. Bake 6 to 8 minutes or until bottoms are lightly browned. Transfer cookies to a wire rack with waxed paper underneath to cool. Repeat with remaining dough.

For icing, combine confectioners sugar, water, corn syrup, and almond extract in a medium bowl; stir until smooth. Transfer 1/4 cup icing into each of 2 small bowls; tint black and yellow. Cover with plastic wrap. Tint remaining icing red. Thin red icing with water, 1/4 teaspoon at a time, until icing is thin enough to flow over cookies. Ice wings with red icing; let icing harden. Ice birds with red icing. Press wings onto birds before icing hardens; let icing harden. Spoon black and yellow icing into pastry bags fitted with small round tips. Pipe black masks and yellow beaks onto birds; let icing harden. Pipe yellow eyes onto birds; let icing harden. Store in a single layer in an airtight container.

Yield: about 2 dozen cookies

Baked in a mini fluted tube pan, these scrumptious Holiday Cherry Cakes fit right in with the spirit of the season. Simple icing leaves and berries add a festive look to the tiny cakes.

HOLIDAY CHERRY CAKES

- 1 package (18 1/4 ounces) cherry cake mix
- 1 package (3.4 ounces) vanilla instant pudding mix
- 4 eggs
- 1 cup water
- 1/3 cup vegetable oil
- 2 packages (4 ounces each) red candied cherries, chopped
- 4 1/2 to 4 3/4 cups confectioners sugar
- 7 tablespoons milk
- 3 tablespoons vegetable shortening
- 2 tablespoons light corn syrup
- 1 teaspoon clear vanilla extract
- 1 tube **each** green and red icing

Preheat oven to 350 degrees. In a large bowl, combine cake mix, pudding mix, eggs, water, and oil; beat 2 minutes or until smooth. Stir in cherries. Spoon 1/2 cup batter into each greased mold of a 6-mold fluted tube pan. Bake 20 to 23 minutes or until a toothpick inserted in center of cake comes out clean. Cool in pan 5 minutes. Remove from pan and cool completely on a wire rack.

In a large bowl, combine confectioners sugar, milk, shortening, corn syrup, and vanilla; beat until smooth. Spoon white icing over tops of cakes; let icing harden. Transfer red and green icing into pastry bags. Use green icing and a small leaf tip to pipe holly leaves onto cakes. Use red icing and a small round tip to pipe berries onto cakes; let icing harden.

Yield: about 2 dozen cakes

LEMON-FILLED CARDINAL CAKE

FILLING

- 1/2 cup sugar
- 1 tablespoon cornstarch
- 1 cup boiling water
- 1 tablespoon grated lemon zest
- 2 tablespoons butter or margarine
- 2 tablespoons freshly squeezed lemon juice

CAKE

- 3/4 cup butter or margarine, softened
- 1 1/2 cups sugar
- 3 eggs
- 2 teaspoons grated lemon zest
- 1 teaspoon vanilla extract
- 1 teaspoon lemon extract
- 2 cups all-purpose flour
- 2 1/2 teaspoons baking powder
- 1/2 teaspoon salt
- 3/4 cup milk

ICING

- 6 cups confectioners sugar
- 1 1/2 cups vegetable shortening
- 5 to 6 tablespoons milk
- 1 teaspoon clear vanilla extract
- 1 teaspoon butter flavoring
- 1/4 teaspoon salt
  Red, green, black, and yellow paste food coloring

For filling, combine sugar and cornstarch in a small saucepan. Add

Surprise guests with a dessert that's as pleasing to the eye as it is to the tummy! Our Lemon-Filled Cardinal Cake features a creamy filling sandwiched with lemony cake layers. Use brightly colored icings to create plaid trim, holly leaves and berries, and a cheerful cardinal.

boiling water and lemon zest. Stirring constantly, bring to a boil over medium heat; boil 5 minutes (mixture will thicken). Remove from heat. Add butter and lemon juice; stir until butter melts. Transfer filling to a heatproof container. Cover and chill 2 hours.

Preheat oven to 375 degrees. For cake, grease two 8-inch square cake pans and line bottoms with waxed paper. In a large bowl, cream butter and sugar until fluffy. Add eggs, lemon zest, and extracts; beat until smooth. In a small bowl, combine flour, baking powder, and salt. Alternately beat dry ingredients and milk into creamed mixture, beating until well blended. Spoon batter into prepared pans. Bake 20 to 25 minutes or until a toothpick inserted in center of cake comes out clean. Cool in pans 10 minutes. Remove from pans and cool completely on a wire rack.

For icing, combine confectioners sugar, shortening, milk, vanilla, butter flavoring,

and salt in a large bowl; beat until well blended and smooth. Transfer 1 1/3 cups icing to a small bowl; cover and reserve for decorating.

To assemble cake, slice layers in half horizontally. Spread filling between each sliced layer. Spread about 1 cup icing on 1 lemon-filled layer; top with remaining lemon-filled layer. Ice top and sides of cake with remaining icing.

To decorate cake, trace bird and holly leaf patterns onto paper; cut out. Place patterns on cake and use a toothpick to draw around patterns; remove patterns. Using reserved 1 1/3 cups icing, place icing in small bowls and tint 3/4 cup red, 1/3 cup green, 2 tablespoons black, and 2 tablespoons yellow. Spoon red, black, and yellow icing into pastry bags fitted with small round tips. Outline and fill in mask with black. Fill in beak and pipe eye with yellow. Outline body of bird with red. Use a medium round tip and red icing to fill in body, smoothing icing with

a small metal spatula. Referring to photo, use small round tip and red icing to pipe outline of wing onto bird. Use a medium round tip and red icing to fill in wing, smoothing icing with spatula.

To decorate sides of cake, spoon green icing into a pastry bag fitted with a medium round tip and place a basketweave tip on red pastry bag. For vertical stripes, use red icing and flat side of a basketweave tip to pipe a vertical stripe from top to bottom of cake. Use green icing to pipe a vertical stripe about 1/2 inch from red stripe. Repeat vertical stripes around sides of cake. For horizontal stripes, pipe red stripes around top, middle, and bottom of cake. Pipe a green stripe around top edge of cake next to red stripe and between middle and bottom red stripes. Store in an airtight container.

Yield: about 16 servings

FONDUE FAVORITES

A popular party trend of years past, fondue is the art of dipping an array of morsels, from appetizers to dessert foods, into scrumptious sauces. We've brought back this fun serving style with recipes for sweet, delectable dips that complement moist pound cakes, fruit chunks, marshmallows, and any other bite-size snacks you choose. What a festive way to share your warm wishes with friends and family this Yuletide season!

Creamy Marshmallow Fondue is a tasty way to add fluffy sweetness to mandarin oranges, pineapple chunks, cherries, and bits of Chocolate Pound Cake Loaf.

Fondue Equipment

There is a wide selection of fondue pots available. You can choose from a variety of materials, sizes, and heat sources. The simplest one is a fondue pot on a stand that uses a special canned or liquid fuel as a heat source. Electric thermostatically controlled pots are also available. These are useful when a controlled heat is needed for a delicate sauce that might scorch or when it is necessary to maintain a high temperature for fried foods. Fondue forks may come with the pot or they can be purchased separately. These long, thin forks (which may be color coded) are useful for dipping or cooking food. Long party-type toothpicks can also be used for dipping when entertaining a large group. Fondue plates with several divided sections are also available.

A definite crowd-pleaser, thick and bubbly Caramel Fondue will be irresistible for dipping with marshmallows and fruit.

CREAMY MARSHMALLOW FONDUE

    1   cup sugar, divided
 1/3   cup water
  20   regular marshmallows
    3   egg whites
    3   tablespoons water
    2   tablespoons light corn syrup
 1/4   teaspoon cream of tartar
    1   teaspoon clear vanilla extract

In a heavy large saucepan, combine 2/3 cup sugar and 1/3 cup water. Stirring frequently, bring to a boil over high heat. Remove from heat. Add marshmallows; stir until melted. Cover marshmallow mixture and set aside.

In top of a double boiler, combine remaining 1/3 cup sugar, egg whites, 3 tablespoons water, corn syrup, and cream of tartar. Beat with an electric mixer until sugar is well blended. Place over simmering water; continue to beat about 7 minutes or until soft peaks form (temperature of mixture should reach 160 degrees). Remove from heat and add vanilla; stir into marshmallow mixture. Serve warm or store in an airtight container in refrigerator.

To reheat, place sauce in a heavy medium saucepan over low heat. Stirring constantly, heat 10 minutes or until heated through. Serve warm.
Yield: about 6 cups sauce

CHOCOLATE POUND CAKE LOAF

    1   cup butter or margarine, softened
1 2/3 cups sugar
    3   eggs
    1   teaspoon vanilla extract
    2   cups all-purpose flour
 1/3   cup cocoa
 1/2   teaspoon baking powder
 1/4   teaspoon salt
 2/3   cup milk

Preheat oven to 325 degrees. Grease a 5 x 9-inch loaf pan. Line bottom of pan with waxed paper; grease waxed paper. In a large bowl, cream butter and sugar until fluffy. Add eggs, 1 at a time, beating well after each addition. Stir in vanilla. In a small bowl, combine flour, cocoa, baking powder, and salt. Alternately beat dry ingredients and milk into creamed mixture, beating until well blended. Spoon batter into prepared pan. Bake 1 1/4 hours or until a toothpick inserted in center of cake comes out clean. Cool in pan 10 minutes. Remove from pan and cool completely on a wire rack. Store in an airtight container.
Yield: 1 loaf cake

CARAMEL FONDUE

    1   cup butter
 1/2   cup water
 1/4   cup light corn syrup
    1   cup firmly packed brown sugar
    1   cup granulated sugar
 1/2   teaspoon salt
 1/2   cup hot whipping cream
    2   teaspoons vanilla extract

In a heavy large saucepan, combine butter, water, and corn syrup. Cook over medium-low heat until butter melts. Add sugars and salt. Stirring constantly, cook until sugars dissolve. Increase heat to medium and bring to a boil. Cook, without stirring, until mixture darkens and thickens (about 10 minutes). Remove from heat. Stirring constantly, slowly add whipping cream; stir until mixture is smooth. Stir in vanilla. Serve warm or transfer to a microwave-safe container. Store in an airtight container in refrigerator.

To reheat, microwave on medium-high power (80%) 4 minutes or until dipping consistency, stirring after 2 minutes. Serve warm.
Yield: about 3 cups sauce

A spirited complement to Vanilla Bean Pound Cake, Grand Marnier Sauce has a smooth, light citrus flavor. Red, ripe strawberries also make perfect partners for this mouth-watering treat.

GRAND MARNIER SAUCE

    3 cups whipping cream
    1 cup sugar
    1 cup orange juice
 1 1/2 tablespoons freshly squeezed
         lemon juice
    2 eggs
    4 egg yolks
  1/4 cup Grand Marnier liqueur

Stirring constantly, bring whipping cream to a boil in a heavy large saucepan over medium-high heat. Reduce heat to medium and cook until volume is reduced by half (about 25 minutes). Add sugar; stir until sugar dissolves. Transfer whipping cream mixture to top of a double boiler over simmering water. Stir in orange juice and lemon juice. In a small bowl, combine eggs and egg yolks; beat until light in color. Stirring constantly, add a small amount of hot mixture to eggs; stir egg mixture back into whipping cream mixture in double boiler. Stirring constantly, cook

about 15 minutes or until mixture coats the back of a spoon. Remove from heat. Pour into a medium heat-resistant bowl in an ice-water bath. Add liqueur; stir frequently until mixture cools (about 10 minutes). Place plastic wrap directly on surface of sauce; refrigerate 2 hours or until well chilled. Serve chilled.
Yield: about 3 2/3 cups sauce

VANILLA BEAN POUND CAKE

    6 tablespoons milk
    1 vanilla bean, split in half
         lengthwise and cut into thirds
    1 cup butter or margarine, softened
    1 cup sugar
    4 eggs
    1 teaspoon vanilla extract
    2 cups all-purpose flour
  3/4 teaspoon baking powder
  1/8 teaspoon salt

Grease a 5 x 9-inch loaf pan. Line bottom of pan with waxed paper; grease waxed paper. Combine milk and vanilla bean pieces in a small saucepan. Stirring constantly, bring milk to a simmer over medium heat. Remove from heat; cover and set aside.

Preheat oven to 325 degrees. In a large bowl, cream butter and sugar until fluffy. Beat in eggs, 1 at a time, beating well after each addition. Add vanilla extract; beat until smooth. In a small bowl, combine flour, baking powder, and salt. Remove vanilla bean pieces from milk and scrape seeds into milk; discard bean pieces. Alternately beat dry ingredients and milk into creamed mixture, beating until well blended. Spoon batter into prepared pan. Bake 1 to 1 1/4 hours or until a toothpick inserted in center of cake comes out clean and top is golden brown. Cool in pan 10 minutes. Remove from pan and cool completely on a wire rack. Store in an airtight container.
Yield: 1 loaf cake

HONEY-CINNAMON COFFEE

1½ tablespoons ground coffee
½ teaspoon ground cinnamon
3 cups water
6 tablespoons honey
¼ cup warm half and half

Combine coffee and cinnamon in a coffee filter. Pour water into a drip coffee maker and brew coffee. Stir honey and half and half into brewed coffee; serve immediately.
Yield: about 3 cups coffee

CHOCOLATE FONDUE

½ cup light corn syrup
½ cup whipping cream
1 package (6 ounces) bittersweet baking chocolate, chopped

In a heavy medium saucepan, combine corn syrup and whipping cream. Bring mixture to a boil over medium heat. Remove from heat and add chocolate; stir until chocolate melts. Serve warm or store in an airtight container in refrigerator.

To reheat, place sauce in a medium microwave-safe bowl and microwave on medium-high power (80%) 2 minutes or until chocolate softens; stir until smooth. Serve warm.
Yield: about 1½ cups sauce

WHITE CHOCOLATE FONDUE

3 cups whipping cream
½ cup sugar
¼ cup white crème de cacao
1½ teaspoons vanilla extract
12 ounces white chocolate, chopped

In a heavy large saucepan, combine whipping cream and sugar over medium heat. Stirring frequently, bring mixture to a boil. Reduce heat to medium low and simmer about 25 minutes or until liquid has been reduced to 2 cups. Remove from heat. Stir in crème de cacao and vanilla. Add white chocolate; stir until melted. Serve warm or store in a microwave-safe container in refrigerator.

To reheat, microwave sauce on medium power (50%) 8 minutes or until smooth, stirring after each minute. Serve warm.
Yield: about 3 cups sauce

Fruit, nuts, pretzels, and cake are fun to dip in easy-to-make Chocolate Fondue and liqueur-flavored White Chocolate Fondue. They taste especially delicious with a cup of steaming Honey-Cinnamon Coffee.

149

YULETIDE REUNION

Reuniting faraway friends around the dinner table for food and fellowship makes for a truly memorable Yuletide event. Even before the first course is served, the house is filled with conversation and laughter as guests renew memories of years past and share the latest news. Photographs are passed around the table along with the bread and wine, and cameras flash as each moment is captured on film. Whether your friends have come from across the country or across the street, their hearts will be warmed by the festive mood and our collection of savory dishes and mouth-watering sweets.

ROASTED RED PEPPER SOUP

- 4 sweet red peppers
- 3 tablespoons butter or margarine
- 1³/₄ cups chopped onions
- ¹/₂ cup sliced carrot
- 3 cloves garlic, minced
- 2 tablespoons all-purpose flour
- 2 cans (14¹/₂ ounces each) chicken broth
- 1 can (14¹/₂ ounces) whole tomatoes
- 1 cup whipping cream
- ¹/₄ cup white wine
- 2 tablespoons freshly squeezed lemon juice
- 1 teaspoon honey
- 1 teaspoon salt
- ¹/₄ teaspoon ground white pepper
  Parsley to garnish

To roast peppers, cut in half lengthwise and remove seeds and membranes. Place, skin side up, on a greased baking sheet; flatten with hand. Broil about 3 inches from heat about 15 to 20 minutes or until skin of peppers blackens. Immediately seal peppers in a plastic bag and allow to steam 10 to 15 minutes. Remove and discard charred skin.

In a large Dutch oven, melt butter over medium heat. Sauté onions, carrot, and garlic about 5 minutes or until onion is tender. Stirring constantly, add flour and cook about 2 minutes. Stir in chicken broth, tomatoes, and peppers; bring to a simmer. Reduce heat to medium low. Stirring occasionally, cover and simmer about 25 minutes or until vegetables are tender. Process mixture in batches in a food processor until vegetables are puréed. Return mixture to Dutch oven. Stir in whipping cream, wine, lemon juice, honey, salt, and white pepper. Cook until heated through (do not boil). Garnish individual servings with parsley, if desired.

Yield: about 7 cups soup

Set the scene for good food and good cheer with your best holiday china and table linens; tie shining ribbon around napkins and goblet stems. Instead of place cards, hang a handmade stocking for each guest and trim it with a colorful glass ornament painted with his or her name; invite everyone to bring little gifts to tuck in the stockings! To complete the setting, fill the table with brilliant poinsettias and add photographs of past gatherings to the arrangement.

Guests can warm up to a bowl of creamy Roasted Red Pepper Soup. Complete the course with homemade Parmesan Cheese Crisps and finish with a glass of spirited Christmas Sangria.

PARMESAN CHEESE CRISPS

These crackers freeze well.

- 1 cup butter, softened
- 1 clove garlic, minced
- 2 cups all-purpose flour
- 1 cup freshly grated Parmesan cheese
- 2 tablespoons dried parsley flakes

Process butter and garlic in a large food processor until smooth. Add flour, Parmesan cheese, and parsley flakes; process until well blended. Shape cheese mixture into two 10-inch-long rolls. Wrap in plastic wrap and chill 2 hours or until firm enough to slice.

Preheat oven to 350 degrees. Cut rolls into ¹/₄-inch slices. Place slices on an ungreased baking sheet. Bake 13 to 15 minutes or until crackers are golden brown. Transfer to a wire rack to cool. Store in an airtight container.

Yield: about 6¹/₂ dozen crackers

CHRISTMAS SANGRIA

- 4 navel oranges, sliced
- 2 lemons, sliced
- 1¹/₂ cups sugar
- 2 bottles (750 ml each) dry white wine, chilled
- 1 can (12 ounces) frozen cranberry juice cocktail concentrate, thawed
- 2 tablespoons orange-flavored liqueur
- 2 tablespoons brandy
- 1 bottle (1 liter) club soda, chilled

Place fruit slices in a large bowl. Pour sugar over fruit; stir with a wooden spoon until fruit is coated with sugar. Cover and let stand at room temperature 1 hour.

In a large container combine fruit mixture, wine, cranberry juice concentrate, liqueur, and brandy. Cover and chill 2 hours.

To serve, transfer wine mixture to a 5-quart serving container; stir in club soda. Serve immediately.

Yield: about 14 cups wine

ELEGANT CRANBERRY SALAD

- 1 can (8 ounces) crushed pineapple in juice
- 1 cup boiling water
- 2 packages (3 ounces each) cranberry gelatin
- 1 cup cold water
- 1 can (16 ounces) whole berry cranberry sauce
- 1 cup chopped walnuts
- 1 cup chopped unpeeled red apple (we used Red Delicious)
- ½ cup finely chopped celery
  Lettuce leaves to serve

Drain pineapple, reserving juice in a measuring cup. Add enough water to juice to make 1 cup. In a medium bowl, stir boiling water into gelatin; stir until gelatin dissolves. Add pineapple juice mixture, cold water, and cranberry sauce; stir until well blended. Chill gelatin mixture about 45 minutes or until partially set, stirring occasionally.

Fold pineapple, walnuts, apple, and celery into gelatin mixture. Pour into a lightly oiled 9 x 13-inch baking dish. Cover and chill about 2 hours or until firm.

Cut gelatin into 3-inch squares. Serve on lettuce leaves.

Yield: about 12 servings

CORN SOUFFLÉS

Soufflés can be made ahead and chilled until ready to bake.

- 1½ cups water
- ¾ cup yellow cornmeal
- 2 cups (8 ounces) shredded sharp Cheddar cheese
- 1 can (11 ounces) whole kernel corn, drained
- 1 small clove garlic, minced
- ½ teaspoon salt
- ⅛ teaspoon ground white pepper
- ¾ cup milk
- 4 eggs, separated

Preheat oven to 325 degrees. In a large saucepan, combine water and cornmeal. Stirring constantly, cook over medium heat 3 to 4 minutes or until mixture thickens. Reduce heat to low. Add cheese, corn, garlic, salt, and white pepper; stir until cheese melts. Remove from heat. In a small bowl, combine milk and egg yolks; beat until blended. Stir into cornmeal mixture. In a medium bowl, beat egg whites until stiff. Fold egg whites

into cornmeal mixture. Spoon into 7 greased 1-cup ramekins. (Mixture may be covered and chilled until ready to bake.) Bake 30 to 35 minutes (40 to 45 minutes if chilled) or until puffed and lightly browned. Serve immediately.

Yield: 7 servings

BRIE-STUFFED CHICKEN BREASTS WITH GREEN PEPPERCORN SAUCE

CHICKEN BREASTS

- 6 boneless, skinless chicken breasts
- ¼ cup mayonnaise

Delight friends with a scrumptious spread of holiday fare. Begin with Elegant Cranberry Salad featuring crunchy celery, walnuts, and chopped apples. A light side dish, time-saving Corn Soufflés can be made ahead and baked just before serving. Our Brie-Stuffed Chicken Breasts with Green Peppercorn Sauce are bursting with the robust flavor of Dijon mustard.

- 2 tablespoons Dijon-style mustard
- ½ teaspoon ground white pepper
- 8 ounces Brie cheese, rind removed and shredded
- ½ cup purchased plain bread crumbs
- ½ cup chopped pecans, toasted and ground
- 1 tablespoon finely chopped fresh parsley

GREEN PEPPERCORN SAUCE

- ¼ cup butter or margarine
- ¼ cup minced onion
- 2 tablespoons green peppercorns, crushed
- 1 can (14½ ounces) chicken broth
- ¼ cup finely chopped fresh parsley

The zesty flavor of Golden Lemon Biscuits (*left*) is enhanced with dollops of Lemon Butter (*recipes on page 154*). A cool and tangy recipe made with red wine vinegar, Marinated Mushrooms (*recipe on page 154*) add vibrant color to the table. Tasty Oven-Roasted Vegetables are delicately seasoned with fresh ginger and thyme for a delicious complement to any meal.

2 tablespoons Dijon-style mustard
³/₄ teaspoon salt
2 cups half and half
2 tablespoons cornstarch
¹/₄ cup water

Preheat oven to 350 degrees. Place chicken between sheets of waxed paper. Using a mallet, gently pound chicken pieces until ¹/₄-inch thick. In a small bowl, combine mayonnaise and mustard. Spread 1 tablespoon mixture over each chicken breast. Sprinkle chicken breasts with white pepper. Place ¹/₄ cup cheese in center of each chicken piece. Beginning at 1 short edge, roll up chicken jellyroll style; secure with a toothpick. (Chicken may be covered and chilled until ready to bake.) In a shallow bowl, combine bread crumbs, pecans, and parsley. Coat chicken with crumb mixture. Place chicken in a lightly greased jellyroll pan. Bake 35 minutes (40 minutes if chilled) or until juices run clear when pierced with a fork.

For green peppercorn sauce, melt butter in a medium saucepan over medium heat. Sauté onion and peppercorns in butter about 5 minutes or until onion is tender; stir in chicken broth. Stirring occasionally, cook mixture 25 minutes or until volume is reduced by half. Add parsley, mustard, and salt; stir until well blended. Stirring frequently, add half and half and bring mixture to a simmer over medium-high heat. In a small bowl, combine cornstarch and water. Stirring constantly, add cornstarch mixture and cook about 1 minute or until sauce is bubbly and thickened. Serve warm or store in an airtight container in refrigerator until ready to serve.

To reheat sauce, place in a medium microwave-safe bowl. Microwave on medium-high power (80%) about 6 minutes or until heated through, stirring every 2 minutes. Remove toothpicks from chicken. Serve ¹/₂ cup sauce with each chicken piece.
Yield: 6 servings

OVEN-ROASTED VEGETABLES

1 package (16 ounces) frozen bean and carrot blend, thawed
1 package (16 ounces) frozen peas with baby corn and snow peas, thawed
³/₄ cup butter or margarine
2 tablespoons freshly grated ginger
1¹/₂ tablespoons finely chopped fresh thyme leaves
1 teaspoon salt
¹/₂ teaspoon ground black pepper
1 jar (15 ounces) whole small onions, drained

Preheat oven to 400 degrees. In a large roasting pan, combine first 2 ingredients. In a small saucepan, combine butter, ginger, thyme, salt, and pepper. Stirring constantly, cook over medium-low heat until butter melts. Pour over vegetables. Bake 30 minutes, stirring after 15 minutes. Stir in onions and bake 15 minutes or until vegetables are tender and lightly browned.
Yield: about 6 cups vegetables

LEMON BUTTER

(Shown on page 153)

- 1/2 cup butter or margarine, softened
- 2 teaspoons freshly squeezed lemon juice
- 1 teaspoon grated lemon zest

In a small bowl, combine butter, lemon juice, and lemon zest; beat until well blended. Cover and store in refrigerator.
Yield: about 1/2 cup butter

GOLDEN LEMON BISCUITS

(Shown on page 153)

- 2 cups all-purpose flour
- 2 tablespoons sugar
- 2 teaspoons baking powder
- 1/2 teaspoon salt
- 1/2 cup chilled butter or margarine
- 2 eggs, beaten
- 3 tablespoons milk
- 2 tablespoons freshly squeezed lemon juice
- 2 teaspoons grated lemon zest

Preheat oven to 400 degrees. In a medium bowl, combine flour, sugar, baking powder, and salt. Using a pastry blender or 2 knives, cut in butter until mixture resembles coarse meal. Stir in eggs, milk, lemon juice, and lemon zest just until blended. On a lightly floured surface, knead dough about 1 minute or until smooth. Roll out dough to 1/2-inch thickness; use a 2-inch biscuit cutter to cut out biscuits. Place biscuits 2 inches apart on an ungreased baking sheet. Bake 12 to 15 minutes or until tops are golden brown. Serve warm with Lemon Butter.
Yield: about 1 1/2 dozen biscuits

MARINATED MUSHROOMS

(Shown on page 153)

- 1 pound fresh mushrooms (we used white, shiitake, and golden Italian)
- 1 bottle (16 ounces) red wine vinegar and oil salad dressing
- 1/4 cup chopped fresh parsley
- 2 tablespoons drained capers

Clean, trim, and slice mushrooms. Place in a medium container. Stir in salad dressing, parsley, and capers. Cover and chill overnight, stirring mushrooms several times. Serve chilled.
Yield: about 4 3/4 cups mushrooms

An eye-catching Yuletide display, our Eggnog Trifle contrasts rich pudding with colorful oranges and cherries, all layered with slices of moist pound cake.

EGGNOG TRIFLE

- 2 packages (3 ounces each) vanilla pudding mix
- 1 carton (1 quart) eggnog
- 1/4 teaspoon freshly grated nutmeg (optional)
- 2 loaves (10 3/4 ounces each) pound cake
- 1/3 cup cream sherry
- 2 1/4 cups whipping cream, divided
- 3 cans (11 ounces each) mandarin oranges, drained
- 1 jar (10 ounces) maraschino cherry halves, drained
- 2 tablespoons confectioners sugar
- 1 teaspoon vanilla extract

Combine pudding mix and eggnog in a medium saucepan. Stirring constantly, cook over medium heat until mixture comes to a full boil. Pour mixture into a large heatproof bowl. Stir in nutmeg, if desired. Place plastic wrap directly on surface of pudding; chill 1 hour.

Cut top of pound cake flat and trim edges from cake. Cut cake into 1/2-inch slices. Place slices on waxed paper. Brush slices with sherry. Beat 1 1/4 cups whipping cream in a medium bowl until stiff peaks form. Fold whipped cream into pudding. Place one-third of cake slices in bottom of a 16-cup trifle bowl. Spoon 2 cups pudding over cake. Using 1 1/2 cups oranges, line outside edge of bowl and place remaining oranges over pudding. Using 1/2 cup cherries, line outside edge of bowl and place remaining cherries over oranges. Continue layering using half of remaining cake, 2 cups pudding, 1 1/2 cups oranges, 1/2 cup cherries, remaining cake, and remaining pudding. Cover and chill until ready to serve.

To serve, beat remaining 1 cup whipping cream, confectioners sugar, and vanilla in a small bowl until stiff peaks form. Spoon whipped cream into a pastry bag fitted with a large star tip. Pipe dollops of whipped cream onto top of trifle.
Yield: about 24 servings

CHOCOLATE PEPPERMINT PATTIES

- 7 cups confectioners sugar
- 7 tablespoons cocoa
- 1 can (14 ounces) sweetened condensed milk
- 1/2 cup butter, softened
- 1 teaspoon peppermint extract
- 24 ounces chocolate candy coating, chopped
- 1 package (12 ounces) semisweet chocolate chips

In a large bowl, combine confectioners sugar and cocoa. Add sweetened condensed milk, butter, and peppermint extract; beat until well blended. Shape mixture into 1-inch balls and flatten each ball to make a 1 1/2-inch-diameter patty. Place patties on baking sheets lined with waxed paper. Freeze patties 30 minutes or until thoroughly chilled.

In top of a double boiler, melt candy coating and chocolate chips over hot, not simmering, water. Remove double boiler from heat. Remove 1 dozen patties at a time from freezer. Placing each patty on a fork and holding over saucepan, spoon chocolate mixture over patties. Return to baking sheets lined with waxed paper. Let chocolate harden. Store in an airtight container in refrigerator.

Yield: about 7 1/2 dozen patties

FAVOR STOCKINGS
(Shown on page 150)

For each stocking, you will need tracing paper, 1/3 yd. of plaid taffeta for stocking, 1 1/4 yds. of 1/8"w gold cord with lip, 1/4 yd. of red velvet for hanger and cuff, pressing cloth, straight pins, gold fine-tip paint pen, red satin glass ornament, and 18" of 1/16"w gold cord.

Note: Match right sides and raw edges and use a 1/2" seam allowance for all sewing unless otherwise indicated. Use pressing cloth for all pressing.

1. Aligning arrows and dotted lines, trace stocking top B and stocking bottom patterns, page 55, onto tracing paper. For seam allowance, draw a second line 1/2" outside the first. Cut out pattern along outer line.
2. Matching short edges, fold taffeta in half. Using pattern, cut out stocking pieces.
3. Matching raw edges on right side of taffeta, baste lip of cord along side and bottom edges of front of stocking.

Refreshing Chocolate Peppermint Patties *(left, on plate)* are a great way to end a satisfying meal. Give each guest a decorated photo album to hold snapshots of the festivities. The memories will last a lifetime!

4. Using a zipper foot and stitching as close to cord as possible, sew stocking pieces together. Clip curves and turn right side out.
5. For hanger, cut a 2 1/4" x 14" strip from velvet. Press long edges 1/2" to wrong side. Matching wrong sides and long edges, press in half; stitch close to pressed edges. Matching short ends, fold hanger in half to form a loop. Matching raw edges, pin loop inside stocking at heel seam.
6. For cuff, cut a 7" x 16" piece from velvet. Sew short edges together; press seam open.
7. Matching wrong sides and raw edges, fold cuff in half. Matching raw edges, place cuff inside top of stocking. Sew cuff to stocking. Turn cuff to outside of stocking.
8. Use gold pen to write name and draw holly leaves and berries on ornament. Use 1/16"w cord to tie ornament to stocking.

FRIENDSHIP PHOTO ALBUM

You will need a 2 1/2" dia. gold frame, 3" square of ecru card stock, black permanent fine-point marker, 18" of 7/8"w red wired ribbon with gold edges, hot glue gun, and a 5" x 6 1/2" photo album.

1. Trace around frame on card stock. Cut out circle just inside drawn line. Use marker to write "Friendship grows from pleasures shared" on circle. Mount circle in frame.
2. Tie ribbon into a bow with 5" streamers. Glue bow and frame to album.

MAKING PATTERNS

When entire pattern is shown, place tracing paper over pattern and trace pattern. For a more durable pattern, use a permanent marker to trace pattern onto stencil plastic.

When pattern pieces are stacked or overlapped, place tracing paper over pattern and follow a single color to trace pattern. Repeat to trace each pattern separately onto tracing paper.

When only half of pattern is shown (indicated by blue line on pattern), fold tracing paper in half and match fold of paper to blue line of pattern. Trace pattern half; turn folded paper over and draw over traced lines on remaining side of paper.

SEWING SHAPES

1. Center pattern on wrong side of one fabric piece and use fabric marking pen to draw around pattern. Do not cut out shape.
2. Place fabric pieces right sides together. Leaving an opening for turning, carefully sew pieces together directly on drawn line.
3. Leaving a 1/4" seam allowance, cut out shape. Clip seam allowance at curves and corners. Turn right side out.

EMBOSSING VELVET

Note: Velvet must be 100% rayon.

1. For each design, trace desired pattern onto tracing paper. Use carbon paper to transfer pattern to linoleum printing block.
2. Use a colored pencil to lightly color in all areas to be cut away.
3. Holding block steady, use a carving tool with a medium U-shaped blade and shallow strokes to make initial cuts and a carving tool with a large U-shaped blade and deep strokes to scoop out colored areas of block. Use a toothbrush to brush away cuttings.
4. For pattern placement, use chalk to mark center of each design on wrong side of velvet.
5. Place block, design side up on flat surface. Place velvet over block, with mark on velvet over center of design. Lightly mist wrong side of velvet with water. Using a hot, dry iron, press velvet for 10 to 15 seconds until impression is made; do **not** slide iron.

MAKING APPLIQUÉS

To prevent darker fabrics from showing through, white or light-colored fabrics may need to be lined with fusible interfacing before applying paper-backed fusible web.

To make reverse appliqué pieces, trace pattern onto tracing paper; turn traced paper over and continue to follow all steps using reversed pattern.

1. Use a pencil to trace pattern or draw around reversed pattern onto paper side of web as many times as indicated for a single fabric. Repeat for additional patterns and fabrics.
2. Follow manufacturer's instructions to fuse traced patterns to wrong side of fabrics. Do not remove paper backing.
3. Cut out appliqué pieces along traced lines. Remove paper backing.
4. Arrange appliqués, web side down, on project, overlapping as necessary. Appliqués can be temporarily held in place by touching appliqués with tip of iron. If appliqués are not in desired position, lift and reposition.
5. Fuse appliqués in place.

CUTTING A FABRIC CIRCLE

1. Cut a square of fabric the size indicated in project instructions.
2. Matching right sides, fold fabric square in half from top to bottom and again from left to right.
3. Tie one end of string to a pencil or fabric marking pen. Measuring from pencil, insert a thumbtack through string at length indicated in project instructions. Insert thumbtack through folded corner of fabric. Holding tack in place and keeping string taut, mark cutting line (**Fig. 1**).

Fig. 1

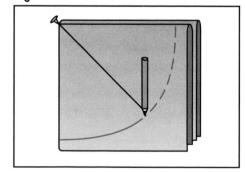

4. Cut along drawn line through all fabric layers.

TEA DYEING

1. Steep one tea bag in two cups hot water; allow to cool. Remove tea bag.
2. Immerse fabric or lace into tea. Soak until desired color is achieved. Remove from tea and allow to dry; press.

MAKING A BOW

Note: Loop sizes given in project instructions refer to the length of ribbon used to make one loop of bow.

1. For first streamer, measure desired length of streamer from one end of ribbon; twist ribbon between fingers (**Fig. 1**).

Fig. 1

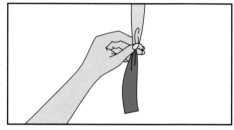

2. Keeping right side of ribbon facing out, fold ribbon to front to form desired-size loop; gather ribbon between fingers (**Fig. 2**). Fold ribbon to back to form another loop; gather ribbon between fingers (**Fig. 3**).

Fig. 2

Fig. 3

3. (**Note:** If a center loop is desired, form half the desired number of loops, then loosely wrap ribbon around thumb and gather ribbon between fingers as shown in **Fig. 4**; form remaining loops.) Continue to form loops, varying size of loops as desired, until bow is desired size.

Fig. 4

4. For remaining streamer, trim ribbon to desired length.

5. To secure bow, hold gathered loops tightly. Fold a length of floral wire around gathers of loops. Hold wire ends behind bow, gathering all loops forward; twist bow to tighten wire. Arrange loops and trim ribbon ends as desired.

MAKING RIBBON ROSES

1. Leaving a ³/₄" tail, fold one end of ribbon length forward (**Fig. 1**). Fold ribbon end in half twice from right to left forming rose center; tack at base (**Fig. 2**).

Fig. 1

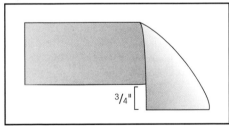

³/₄"

Fig. 2

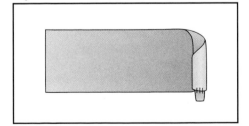

2. Fold ribbon length to back at a right angle. (Increase length of ribbon between fold and rose center to make larger petals.) Roll rose along ribbon length, then around corner of fold (**Fig. 3**), stopping when base of rose lines up with ribbon length; tack in place. Continue folding, rolling, and tacking to add petals (**Fig. 4**) until rose is desired shape.

Fig. 3

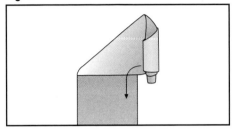

Fig. 4

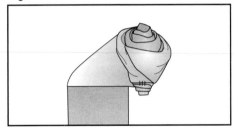

3. Leaving a 2" tail, trim ribbon; gather and tack to base of rose.

PAINTING TECHNIQUES

PREPARING PROJECT
If painting on a garment, wash, dry, and press garment according to paint manufacturer's recommendations. Insert T-shirt form or iron shiny side of freezer paper to wrong side of garment under area to be painted.

TRANSFERRING PATTERNS
Trace pattern onto tracing paper. Using removable tape, tape pattern to project. Place transfer paper coated side down between project and tracing paper (using old transfer paper will help prevent smudges). If transferring pattern onto a dark surface, use light-colored transfer paper to transfer pattern. Use a pencil to transfer outlines of base coat areas of design to project (press lightly to avoid smudges and heavy lines that are difficult to cover). If necessary, use a soft eraser to remove any smudges.

PAINTING BASE COATS
(**Note:** A disposable plate makes a good palette.) Use medium round brush for large areas and a small round brush for small areas. Do not overload brush. Let paint dry between coats.

TRANSFERRING DETAILS
To transfer detail lines to design, replace pattern and transfer paper over painted base coats and use stylus to lightly transfer detail lines onto project.

PAINTING DETAILS
Side loading (shading and highlighting): Dip one corner of a flat brush in water; blot on a paper towel. Dip dry corner of brush into paint. Stroke brush back and forth on palette until there is a gradual change from paint to water in each brush stroke. Stroke loaded side of brush along detail line on project, pulling brush toward you and turning project if necessary. For shading, side load brush with a darker color of paint. For highlighting, side load brush with lighter color of paint.
Line work: Let paint dry before beginning line work to prevent smudging lines or ruining pen. Draw over detail lines with permanent pen.
Dots: Dip the tip of a round paintbrush, the handle end of a paintbrush, or one end of a toothpick in paint and touch to project. Dip in paint each time for uniform dots.
Sponge painting: Lightly dampen sponge piece. Dip sponge piece into paint and blot on paper towel to remove excess paint. Use a stamping motion to apply paint. Reapply paint to sponge as necessary.

WEATHERED WHITEWASH TECHNIQUE
Note: Allow paint and wax to dry between applications and before sanding.

Use fine-grit sandpaper to smooth rough areas on wood; remove dust with tack cloth. Base coat wood with dark brown acrylic paint. For "worn" areas on finished piece, randomly apply paste floor wax to wood. Use antique white acrylic to paint wood piece. Use sandpaper to remove paint over waxed areas.

GENERAL INSTRUCTIONS (continued)

CROCHET

ABBREVIATIONS

ch(s)   chain
Rnd(s) Round(s)
sl st   slip stitch
sc   single crochet
sp(s)   space(s)
st(s)   stitch(es)
YO   yarn over

★- work instructions following ★ as many more times as indicated in addition to the first time.
() or []-work enclosed instructions as many times as specified by the number immediately following or contains explanatory remarks.

SLIP STITCH (sl st): To work a slip stitch, insert hook in stitch indicated, YO and draw through stitch **and** loop on hook (**Fig. 1**). To join with a slip stitch, begin with a slip knot on hook, insert hook in stitch indicated, YO and draw through stitch and through the slip knot on hook.

Fig. 1

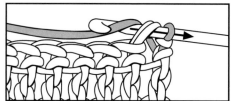

SINGLE CROCHET (sc): To work a single crochet, insert hook in stitch or space indicated, YO and pull up a loop, YO and draw yarn through both loops on hook (**Fig. 2**).

Fig. 2

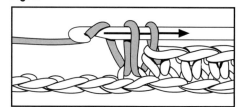

CROSS STITCH

COUNTED CROSS STITCH (X): Work one Cross Stitch for each colored square on chart. For horizontal rows, work stitches in two journeys (**Fig. 1**). For vertical rows, complete each stitch as shown in **Fig. 2**. When the chart shows a Backstitch crossing a colored square (**Fig. 3**), work the Cross Stitch first, then work the Backstitch over the Cross Stitch.

Fig. 1

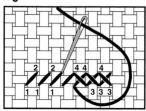

Fig. 2

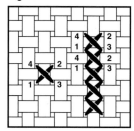

Fig. 3

QUARTER STITCH (¼X): Quarter Stitches are shown as triangular shapes of color in chart and color key. Come up at 1 (**Fig. 4**), then split fabric thread to take needle down at 2.

Fig. 4

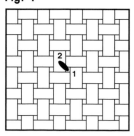

BACKSTITCH (B'ST):

For outline or details, Backstitch (shown in chart and color key by colored straight lines) should be worked after the design has been completed (**Fig. 5**).

Fig. 5

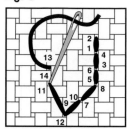

EMBROIDERY STITCHES

BACKSTITCH

Bring needle up at 1; go down at 2. Bring needle up at 3 and back down at 1 (**Fig. 1**). Continue working to make a continuous line of stitches.

Fig. 1

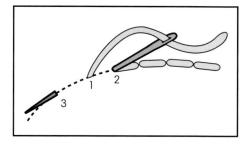

BLANKET STITCH

Bring needle up at 1; keeping thread below point of needle, go down at 2 and up at 3 (**Fig. 2**). Continue working as shown in **Fig. 3**.

Fig. 2

Fig. 3

CROSS STITCH

Bring needle up at 1 and go down at 2. Come up at 3 and go down at 4 (**Fig. 4**).

Fig. 4

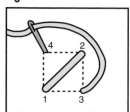

FRENCH KNOT

Bring needle up at 1. Wrap thread once around needle and insert needle at 2, holding thread with non-stitching fingers (**Fig. 5**). Tighten knot as close to fabric as possible while pulling needle back through fabric.

Fig. 5

LAZY DAISY

Bring needle up at 1 and go down at 2 to form a loop; bring needle up at 3, keeping thread below point of needle (**Fig. 6**). Go down at 4 to anchor loop (**Fig. 7**).

Fig. 6

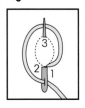

Fig. 7

OVERCAST STITCH

Bring needle up at 1; take thread over edge of fabric and bring needle up at 2. Continue stitching along edge of fabric (**Fig. 8**).

Fig. 8

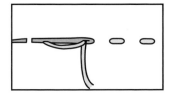

RUNNING STITCH

Make a series of straight stitches with stitch length equal to the space between stitches (**Fig. 9**).

Fig. 9

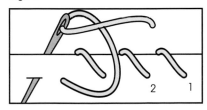

STEM STITCH

Bring needle up at 1. Keeping thread below stitching line, go down at 2 and up at 3. Go down at 4 and up at 5 (**Fig. 10**).

Fig. 10

STRAIGHT STITCH

Bring needle up at 1 and take needle down at 2 (**Fig. 11**). Length of stitches may be varied as desired.

Fig. 11

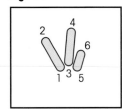

RIBBON EMBROIDERY

CHAIN STITCH

Bring needle up at 1 and down at 2 leaving a loop on top of fabric. Bring needle back up at 3. Go back down at 4 and up at 5 (**Fig. 1**) to make another loop. End chain by bringing needle up through last loop and back down just outside of loop.

Fig. 1

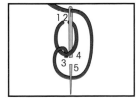

FLY STITCH

Bring needle up at 1; go down at 2 and come up at 3, keeping ribbon below point of needle. Take needle back down at 4 (**Fig. 2**).

Fig. 2

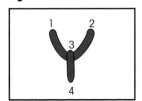

TWISTED STRAIGHT STITCH

Bring needle up at 1, twist ribbon once, and take needle down at 2 (**Fig. 3**).

Fig. 3

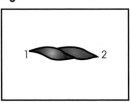

SPIDER WEB ROSE

For anchor stitches, work a Fly Stitch (**Fig. 2**) and add a straight stitch of equal length on each side of the 3-4 stitch. (**Fig. 4**). For ribbon petals, bring needle up at center of anchor stitches; weave ribbon over and under anchor stitches (**Fig. 5**), keeping ribbon loose and allowing ribbon to twist. Continue to weave ribbon until anchor stitches are covered. Take needle down to wrong side of fabric.

Fig. 4

Fig. 5

JAPANESE RIBBON STITCH

Bring needle up at 1. Lay ribbon flat on fabric and take needle down at 2, piercing ribbon (**Fig. 6**). Gently pull needle through to back. Ribbon will curl at end of stitch as shown in **Fig. 7**.

Fig. 6

Fig. 7

CREDITS

We want to extend a warm *thank you* to the generous people who allowed us to photograph our projects at their homes.

- *Make an Entrance:* John and Anne Childs, David and Christine Jernigan, Casey and Wendy Jones
- *Cooking Up Christmas Fun:* William and Nancy Appleton
- *A Victorian Collection:* Scott and Sharon Mosley
- *Redwork Revival:* Duncan and Nancy Porter
- *Nature's Glory:* Tom and Barbara Denniston
- *Keep Christmas in Your Heart:* Rusty and Rhonda Compton
- *Good Tidings:* John and Anne Childs
- *Crimson and Ice:* Mr. and Mrs. Phillip Duncan
- *Candlelight Creole Dinner:* Dr. Dan and Sandra Cook
- *Yuletide Reunion:* Shirley Held
- *The Sharing of Christmas (Snowman Dress, page 98):* Paul and Ann Weaver

To Magna IV Color Imaging of Little Rock, Arkansas, we say thank you for the superb color reproduction and excellent pre-press preparation.

Our sincere appreciation goes to photographers Ken West, Larry Pennington, Mark Mathews, Karen Shirey, and David Hale, Jr., of Peerless Photography, Little Rock, Arkansas; and Jerry R. Davis of Jerry Davis Photography, Little Rock, Arkansas, for their time, patience, and excellent work.

We would like to recognize Viking Husqvarna Sewing Machine Company of Cleveland, Ohio, for providing the sewing machines used to make many of our projects.

To the talented people who helped in the creation of the following projects in this book, we extend a special word of thanks.

- *Santa Patches*, page 109: Kooler Design Studio
- *Crocheted Vest*, page 112: Margie Wicker
- *Poinsettia Afghan* and *Poinsettia Pillow*, page 113: Nancy Overton

We are sincerely grateful to the people who assisted in making and testing the projects in this book: Kandi Ashford, Alice Crowder, Lavonne Sims, and Glenda Taylor.